FOSTER CARE LAW
A Primer

D1713987

FOSTER CARE LAW
A Primer

Harvey Schweitzer, J.D.
Lecturer in Law
Columbus School of Law
The Catholic University of America

Judith Larsen, J.D.
Child and Family Advocate

CAROLINA ACADEMIC PRESS
Durham, North Carolina

Library of Congress-in-Publication Data

Schweitzer, Harvey.
    Foster care law : a primer / by Harvey Schweitzer and Judith Larsen.
        p. cm.
    Includes bibliographical references and index.
    ISBN 0-89089-321-7
    1. Foster home care--Law and legislation--United States. I. Larsen, Judith. II. Title.

    KF3736.5.S39 2004
    344.7303'2733--dc22

                                                            2004016175

Carolina Academic Press
700 Kent Street
Durham, North Carolina 27701
Telephone (919) 489-7486
Fax (919) 493-5668
E-mail: cap@cap-press.com
www.cap-press.com

Printed in the United States of America.

To my wife Sherry and my daughter Hanna
H.S.

...and to Chante, Josephine, and Monica.
J.L.

CONTENTS

Acknowledgments

Heartfelt thanks to readers of our manuscript who took time out of demanding professional schedules to make *Foster Care Law: a Primer* a better book: Professor Daniel Pollack of Yeshiva University, Professor Justine Dunlap of the New England School of Law, and Ellen Manning, M.S.W. A lawyer who did double-duty for us by both critically reading and editing the text is Diane Boyd Rauber, J.D. We are grateful to attorneys Laura Flegel and Patrick Wojahn from the Whitman Walker Clinic in Washington D.C. who researched the rights of a foster child to prevent disclosure of HIV status in court. We are pleased to recognize swift responses to our legal questions from Howard Davidson and Mark Hardin at the American Bar Association Center on Children and the Law, Emily Cooke of the HHS Children's Bureau and Pamela Green-Smith from HHS' Office of Refugee Resettlement. Our thanks to Kathleen Lewis for proficient cite checking. We also thank the Child Welfare League of America for permission to reprint the "Checklist of Needed Services for Children in Foster Care," from Batistelli's Making Managed health Care Work.

Introduction

Foster Care Law: A Primer gives an overview of legal issues to:

Social service professionals who work with children and their families in the foster care system;

Attorneys just entering the foster care field who need to understand the legal relationships between the numerous organizations they will encounter, and the legal issues that may arise;

Graduate social work students researching or interning in the foster care system;

Law students in a juvenile or neglect-abuse clinic, or a family law seminar;

Child advocates who may not be attorneys or social workers but who participate in the court process and negotiate with all parties in a foster care case; and

Graduate public policy students researching the interrelationships among human services entities.

Other persons who may well make use of this book are *judges* who are newly assigned to foster care cases, and the occasional *foster parents* or *biological parents* who are especially intent upon understanding their rights and responsibilities.

There are two main ways to use the book. One could read it straight through to get an overview of all of the issues. Each chapter describes the foster care field from the point of view of one main group: foster parents, foster children, biological parents, public agencies, private agencies, and the court. Appendices show how a case moves through the foster care system, and offers resources for those who wish to go deeper into particular issues.

A second way to use the book is to research a particular problem. For example: an attorney representing a foster care agency that has been sued because a foster child was injured in one of the agency's foster homes could use the liability appendix to orient herself to the major legal issues. That would be her starting point for further legal research in state law.

A supervisor in a private foster care agency might have a policy conflict with the public agency contractor. He could read the chapters on public and private agencies to find out whether there are documents and laws that set forth the two agencies' responsibilities. He would discover in the *Primer* that the contract controls the relationship.

A social worker responsible for recruiting and training foster care parents might want to give the most accurate information about the responsibility split between the foster parents and the foster care agency. She would read the chapters on foster parents and public (or private) agencies.

A master's level social work student could use the *Primer* as a starting point for research on a paper about foster children's rights.

A law student child advocate in a juvenile clinic, up against a seasoned defense attorney in a complex case, could benefit from reading the chapters on both the child's and the biological parents' rights.

Foster care law is extraordinarily complex and much of it is unwritten. That is one reason why there is so little research material available. *Foster Care Law: A Primer* is a start for those professionals and students who need an overview of the whole foster care legal system. It will not answer questions about specific cases, which nearly always grow out of state statutes and case law. It will give the reader a running start.

Harvey Schweitzer, J.D.
Lecturer in Law
Columbus School of Law
Catholic University of America

Judith Larsen, J.D.
Child and Family Advocate

FOSTER CARE LAW
A Primer

Foster Children

CHAPTER GUIDE

I. Overview

Children in foster care are in legal limbo. Because of their age they are not able to independently advocate for protections. Some adults have taken up the cause of children usually as part of class action suits in federal court against foster care agencies. These lawsuits have not won children any new rights, but have at the most enforced some existing legal rights.[1] Moreover, when issues pertaining to children have come to the U.S. Supreme Court, economic interests sometimes win out over the best interests of the child. E.g. *Deshaney v. Winnebago County Social Service Dept.,*489 U.S. 189 (1989).

A child in foster care is torn between the legal interests of at least three groups: parents, the foster care agency that typically has legal custody, and the foster parents who have physical custody. The child cannot choose to visit her parents—that decision is in the hands of the court, the foster care agency, and her parents. The child cannot obtain health care without permission of the social service agency. Daily details of her life are determined by the stranger foster parents into whose home she has been thrust.

As her case moves through the neglect-abuse court, the foster child is a witness to her fate rather than a prime mover. She *may* be asked by a judge to express an opinion about where she wishes to live or go to school. Very often she is not asked. Unless she has vigorous legal representation, her concerns may never be heard. At the end of the year allotted by *The Adoption and Safe Families Act* (ASFA), P.L. 105-89, 42 U.S.C. 620-679, she may be severed from her biological family altogether without the right to choose reunification with her family or to select her new parents. Once her parents' rights to raise her have been terminated, she may be left with no parent at all but the foster care agency.

The rights that foster children do have include health care (usually through Medicaid), a free and appropriate education, and privacy. These rights will be beyond a child's reach, however, unless there is an adult who recognizes them as rights and is willing to pursue them. A good social worker, guardian *ad litem* or other court appointed advocate, foster parent, concerned parent, or astute judge can do that. Often, however, a few rights are secured but many are left unclaimed. For example, a child might have an initial health screening before entering foster care, but may never have needed orthodontics. A child may go to school, but never receive the special education required to overcome developmental delays.

A. Who are Foster Children?

The term "foster child" is not synonymous with an abandoned, abused, or neglected child. Foster care status often occurs before any judicial finding of harm to the child. From a federal perspective, a child becomes a "foster child" by entering full-time out-of-home care under supervision of a state agency. Federal regulations to Title IV-E of the Social Security Act, define "foster care" as:

> …24 hour substitute care for children placed away from their parents and guardians and for whom the state agency has placement and care responsibility. [45 C.F.R. §1355.20]

That out-of-home care could be in:

- foster family homes
- foster homes of relatives
- group homes
- emergency shelters
- residential facilities
- child care institutions
- preadoptive homes

or other settings. A child could be in foster care even if the facility had not received a state license, and maintenance payments came just from state funds, although a fiscally responsible agency wanting federal matching funds would seek to meet federal standards by putting children in licensed facilities. 42 U.S.C. § 672; 45 C.F.R. §1355.20(a). State law can define foster care differently, but the federal definition will always govern distribution of federal funds.

A child usually enters foster care in one of two ways. First, a court can order that it is "contrary to the welfare of the child" to return home after the child has been removed without parental or legal guardian consent. 42 U.S.C. §672(a)(1). In that instance, the family is summoned to court, usually between 24 and 72 hours after the removal (depending on state law), and the "contrary to welfare" order that releases Title IV-E funds is issued at that initial hearing. 45 C.F.R. §1356.21(c).

Alternatively, the parents or legal guardian can conclude a voluntary placement agreement with the state agency that administers the Title IV-E funds. 42 U.S.C. §672. Federal foster care funds can be used for up to 180 days without a court order, but within that time, if the child is not reunited with the family according to conditions in the agreement, a court must hear the case and issue a "contrary to the welfare of the child" order to release more funds. 42 U.S.C. §672. Then the voluntary case is treated just like the involuntary cases, and follows the ASFA schedule of events leading to either reunification with the family or another permanent disposition.

A third way a child can enter foster care is as an "unaccompanied minor," arriving in the United States as a refugee. The Homeland Security Act transferred care for these children to the U.S. Department of Health and Human Services (HHS). Once in foster care, these children are subject to the state's child welfare plan and appear in court on an ASFA schedule. 45 C.F.R. Part 400, Subpart H.

In sum, a foster child simply is a "dependent" child, one who is in 24-hour out-of-home care, receiving services provided by a state agency. Federal law defines dependent child as one who receives foster care maintenance payments and would have been considered a dependent child under the former Aid for Dependent Children statute. 42 U.S.C. § 672. The length of time a child can be in foster care is governed by ASFA, as described in section II.A.1 of this chapter, and time limits on aging out of the foster care system are discussed in section II.F of this chapter.

B. Who Makes Decisions For a Child in Foster Care?

A child has legal ties to three entities: the biological parents, the government agency (public foster care), and the foster parents. All three of those entities claim some rights to control what happens to the child. Although the public foster care agency usually has the dominant legal relationship, the depth of its rights to direct the child's care can vary from state to state (depending on how the state structures its child welfare services), and from child to child (depending on whether a child is receiving foster care services directly from the state agency, or from other delegated or contracted agencies). If the public foster care agency has legal custody, it has the legal right to make many of the big, life-affecting decisions: what kind of facility the child will stay in, where health care will be obtained, whether or not medical procedures can be undertaken, where the child shall go to school, and so forth. With legal custody that agency also would be in charge of developing a case plan for the child that will carry great weight in the ultimate decision about whether the child returns home or moves on to another permanent placement. If legal custody is held by a private agency under contract to the public foster care agency, some of the power to decide what happens to the child could be carried by that private custodial agency, but only as supervised by the public agency, which retains "care and responsibility" functions. U.S. Department of Health and Human Services Children's Bureau Policy 8.3A.12.

The foster parents have physical custody of the child along with the legal obligation to make day-to-day decisions like getting the child to appointments and providing food and shelter. So in that limited sense, the foster parents behave like parents, as described in Chapter Two. The biological parents, who have had to give up physical and legal custody, still maintain something mysteriously called "residual parental rights." These are described in Chapter Three, and at a minimum include visitation, and perhaps some health, religion, and education decisions.

Although, while in custody, the child is mostly within the legal ambit of the public foster care agency, the agency-foster child legal relationship is not equivalent to the parent -child relationship. One could not argue that employees of the agency could act like biological parents and treat the foster child as if she were their own child. For example, an agency usually would not have the authority on its own, without court permission, to withhold life support. A bureaucratic entity can never be a parent to a child in any meaningful sense. However, there are some situations in which the agency holds rights similar, if not almost identical, to the kind of rights that biological parents would otherwise have. This situation could occur, for instance, if the parental rights were terminated and legal custody with the right to consent to adoption had been transferred to the agency by statute or judicial action.

What kind of decisions does a judge make for a child whose foster care case is before the court? Depending on the state in which the case is heard, a judge's influence can range from simply deciding whether neglect or abuse occurred, to prescribing most services and directing the case outcome. In most states a judge can order basic services, such as an initial health screening, especially if the agency has failed to provide them. In a few states judges have a legal basis for ordering almost any service for the child and her family. Case law, statutes, and court rules in other states close the door on judicial discretion to order services from, or payment to, a particular individual, family, or institution—for example, the Wilson foster family or the Happy Days Residential Home or Dr. James Jones. (Chapter Six, section II.A. addresses the subject of judicial discretion.).

How do a child's opinions get expressed to a court and how can a child influence the process and outcome of a case? In a predictable, consistent way, only through the engine of legal representation. The child often cannot participate in the proceedings as fully as the parents. A child is more like the victim in a criminal case, the subject whose harm is central to the case and who can be called to testify. But without legal representation, or a guardian *ad litem's* or child advocate's voice for best interests, the child has limited power to affect the outcome. (See II.B of this chapter)

How many points of contact are there between a judge and a child in a neglect-abuse case? In every state cases flow through the court system in a pattern determined by federal law. There is an initial hearing, trial or stipulation, disposition, review, permanency hearing and ultimate placement. (See Chapter VI, Court Process for a full description). There can be great differences, however, in areas that the federal law has not preempted. The outcome of a child's case can be determined by the way the court conducts its business, influenced by court rules and impacted by state case law. If a child has legal representation and the judge has discretion to influence decisions about medical providers, tests to be administered, schools to be attended, and foster care placements, then the judge's power "trumps" the state agency's power, at least for those issues that are presented to the court. The judge becomes the supervisor of the supervising agency. Therefore, whether the judge or social worker has the dominant influence over what happens to the child may depend on the state in which the child's case is heard. Judicial intervention can be a powerful influence in a foster child's life.

II. Significant Legal Issues

A. Family Reunification v. Other Permanent Placements

Do children have a right to be raised in a certain way? The very question strikes us as odd. We are able to talk about parents' rights to raise their children, or participate in their lives, but children have never been accorded legal rights of the same magnitude. We permit children of a certain maturity to have a "say" in where they shall live, but with very rare exceptions they have no legal right to reclaim their parents or acquire new parents on their own.

The most life-changing legal issue for foster children usually is whether they will return to their parents or be raised in another home in the care of other people. ASFA is the umpire of this issue. Through a combination of ASFA legislation, court improvement funds, and accessible technical resources, each state has refashioned its laws - and more importantly its practices—to acknowledge that children should be headed for a permanent placement within 12 months of their entry into foster care. 42 U.S.C. § 675(5). A defining theme in ASFA is that a child needs a safe permanent home. 42 U.S.C. §671(a)(15). While some state cases have attempted to describe the elements of a safe place, neither ASFA nor its federal regulations do that. Safety is more a placement goal than an enforceable right. ASFA does contain, however, a specific process to achieve permanency.

1. The twelve-month permanency clock

According to ASFA, once the court's first action occurs (for example, a shelter care hearing), progress through foster care should follow a general path. First, a judge makes a preliminary finding that there is probable cause to believe the child has been abused or neglected according to state law definitions, and returning home would be contrary to the child's welfare. 45 C.F.R. §1356. In most states, this initial finding is when the 12-month permanency clock begins to tick. 42 U.S.C. §675(5).

During the ensuing year, the work of the foster care agency and the court intertwine. Ideally, the foster care agency is providing an array of social services to the family to stabilize and rehabilitate members so that the child can return home. 42 U.S.C. § 629a(a). ASFA encourages the agency to make concurrent efforts to develop an alternative permanent placement in case the family cannot be reunified. 42 U.S.C. § 671(a)(15).

Meanwhile, the court case proceeds through trial (or stipulated agreement), disposition, possibly additional court reviews, and ultimately to the twelve-month permanency hearing. At the permanency hearing, the foster care agency presents its permanency plan that recommends either reunification, adoption, legal guardianship, kinship care (placement with relatives), or independent living. 42 U.S.C. § 675(5)(c). In the case of adoption, the legal connection between the child and biological parents is severed either by consent or a court order that terminates parental rights.

Through ASFA, judges and social workers can speed up or slow down the process for developing another permanent placement. Adoption can be accelerated if social services aimed at reunification do not need to be offered to the family, such as where a parent has committed or aided commission of a violent crime, or has abandoned the child. 42 U.S.C. §§671(a)(15). Also, if a child has been involuntarily and permanently removed from a family, reunification services need not be offered in a subsequent sibling's case. 42 U.S.C. §671(a)(15)(D)(iii). Eliminating services should considerably shorten the time it takes for a case to move to termination of parental rights. In addition, some states have taken advantage of ASFA's permission to tighten timelines even more, for example by putting infants and young children on a fast track toward adoption (as in California) or by starting the twelve-month permanency clock running from the date the child was removed from the home, rather than from the date of the judge's first order. 42 U.S.C. §675(5).

On the other hand, the twelve-month permanency clock can be stopped for temporary periods, or even altogether. If a child in foster care returns to the family for a trial home visit, the twelve-month clock is stopped, though it must start again in six months unless a judge's order extends the date. 45 C.F.R. §1356.21(e). Placement with other family members, unless they have been formally designated as foster parents and receive Title IV-E foster care payments, also takes the child's case off the clock. Despite an inability to reunify a child with the parents, if the court agrees that the foster care agency has documented a "compelling reason" why legally severing the parental relationship through a termination of parental rights (TPR) is not in the child's best interests, then adoption need not proceed on that twelve-month time frame. 42 U.S.C. §675(5); 45 C.F.R. §1356(i). An example of a "compelling reason" might be that a biological parent has nearly completed drug treatment but needs a bit more time before reunification can be tried. Or, a sixteen- year old child may have maintained a relationship with her biological parents, despite living with foster parents who are willing to care for, but not adopt, her.

Some state laws and some cases have tried to define "compelling reason," but many states have left it open as urged by the federal government in its preamble to the ASFA regulations, so that in the rare case where it is necessary, the judge would have discretion to fashion an appropriate disposition. 65 F.R. 4058-59 (Jan. 25, 2000).

2. Kinds of placements

The desirable environment that ASFA describes is one that enhances the child's safety and health. 42 U.S.C. §671(a)(15). The implicit hierarchy of placement preferences created by ASFA is based on their potential for permanency. Parents have a relatively short time—basically twelve months—to prove that they can offer their child a safe, healthy, nurturing permanent home.

From the ASFA point of view, *adoption* is considered the most desirable placement if families cannot rehabilitate and reorganize in that short time. That is because adoption is nearly irrevocable, providing a child with the greatest assurance of a permanent home. 42 U.S.C. §§670-679.[2]

Kinship care (a term referring to a child's placement with relatives) is high on the acceptability list if the home is demonstrated to be safe. The preference is for kinship placements to occur through adoption. 42 U.S.C. §671(a)(19).

Legal guardianship was an option that few states offered when ASFA was promulgated, but many states have now rushed to create this permanency tool. 42 U.S.C. §675(7). E.g. Cal. Welf.& Inst. Code § 11405. Legal guardianship transfers to the caretaker those major decisions on health, education, and so forth that were the duties of the foster care agency, and previously, the parents. 45 C.F.R. §1355.20a. *Standby guardianship* is now offered by about half the states, with more laws enacted every year. Standby guardians are especially helpful when a parent is seriously ill, but wishes to maintain the parenting function as long as possible. The standby guardian is a legal guardian "in waiting." ASFA, Section 403, P.L.105-89, "sense of Congress" provision at § 403. (For a good state statute see Ill. Comp. Stat. Ann. 5/11-5-3.)

For youth sixteen or older, none of those options may be as desirable as *living independently* in a supervised and service-supported environment. Some states offer that option. (See Section II.F on "Aging Out")

B. Right to Representation in Court

There is no U.S. Supreme Court case requiring legal representation for neglected or abused children. By contrast, juveniles who face incarceration have a right to legal representation. The difference is that juveniles are at risk to lose liberty, a protected interest under the Constitution. *In re Gault,*387 U.S. 1 (1967).

The only federal statute addressing legal representation for children is *The Child Abuse Prevention and Treatment Act* (CAPTA) P.L. 100-294, 102 Stat.102 (1988), 42 U.S.C. §5106, amended 1996 and 2003 in P.L.108-36. That law approaches the issue indirectly, phrasing it as an eligibility requirement: if a state is to receive demonstration and operation grants under the Act, it must indicate in the state plan certain improvements it intends to carry out, including:

> ...provisions and procedures requiring that in every case involving an abused or neglected child which results in a judicial proceeding, a guardian ad litem who has received training appropriate to the role, who may be an attorney or a court appointed special advocate who has received training appropriate to that role (or both), shall be appointed to represent the child in such proceedings—
>
> > (I) to obtain first-hand, a clear understanding of the situation and needs of the child; and
> >
> > (II) to make recommendations to the court concerning the best interests of the child.

In other words, in order to receive funds under CAPTA, a state must establish a standard for attorney or guardian representation. Not every state receives CAPTA funds, though almost all do. Quite apart from CAPTA, however, every state has at least the potential for representation of children in court. Certain states have chosen not to provide attorney or guardian representation for all children, but only for children whose legal or social needs are apparent. Some states do not provide representation at all stages of the case, but only at points that are considered critical. At the other end of the scale are courts that often provide both an attorney and either a guardian *ad litem* or child advocate when the child's legal interests and "best interests" diverge. Availability of funds can dictate decisions about the kind and extent of representation for children. Compare Cal. Welf.& Inst. § 317 with D.C. Code §16-2304. To understand a court's stance on this issue, one must often look beyond court rules and state statutes to observe court practices.

Whether representation is by an attorney or by a guardian *ad litem* can make a significant difference in the case. An attorney's duty is to pursue a legal strategy on behalf of the child, make motions, participate in discovery, argue the case, and appeal issues as necessary. An attorney has a confidential relationship with the child and, to the extent possible considering age and stage of development, works to achieve the legal goals the child wants. A guardian *ad litem*'s duty is to determine what the child's "best interests" are, and to report those to the court. Though both are working to advance the interests of the child, the attorney works for the child; the guardian *ad litem* works for the court. This difference in point of view can mean that attorneys and guardians *ad litem* can raise and advocate for different issues. See American Bar Association Standards of Practice for Lawyers Representing a Child in Abuse and Neglect Cases, definitions of "The child's attorney" at A-1 and "Lawyer Appointed as Guardian Ad Litem" at A-2. http://www.abanet.org/child/rep-define.html. Court rules may also encourage or discourage participation of a guardian *ad litem* in the legal business of discovery, motions, and appeals. (See discussion, Chapter Six, I.A.)

C. Access to Health Care

1. Laws

There are certain health services to which every foster child is entitled. In the broadest sense, those services are established by federal laws, almost all of them aspects of the Social Security Act. Services are described in these laws and the regulations that interpret them: Early and Periodic Screening, Diagnostic and Treatment Services (EPSDT), 42 U.S.C. §1396d(r)); Medicaid (Title XIX of Social Security Act, §§1396 *et. seq* (1992), and the State Children's Health Insurance Program (SCHIP), Balanced Budget Act of 1997, P.L.105-33, §§4901-23, 111 Stat. 251 (1997) laws and regulations. Foster children funded under Title IV-E of the Social Security Act automatically qualify for Medicaid. Within Medicaid, states are given some discretion about the kind and extent of services, so state laws often do not mirror federal laws. Medicaid provisions, including EPSDT, may be found in a variety of places in state laws, for example, scattered among laws affecting several different state agencies or clustered under program names.

A gateway to foster child health care is EPSDT. This remarkable program, which is part of the Medicaid law, permits children through the age of eighteen to receive routine, thorough medical screening for health problems, as well as diagnoses and "medically necessary" follow-up treatment. It covers compensation for hearing aids, dental care, glasses, as well as medical aspects of mental health care, special education, and more. The federal EPSDT program as it is interpreted by state law often is found under other names, for example, Child and Teen Checkup Screenings (MN), TH Steps (TX), and Health Check (WI). Some states have made a good faith effort to enact the federal mandates, while others have fallen short, often because of shrinking budgets or poorly drafted statutory language. Attorneys, guardians, or social workers advocating for a child's health services may find themselves in the challenging situation of arguing that a court should look to federal law that is specific in its service descriptions, rather than to a vague state law. To buttress this position it is important to focus on the language in Part (5) of the EPSDT law that the described services must be provided "whether or not such services are covered under the state plan." The Sixth Circuit Court of Appeals has ruled that state officials may be sued in federal court for failing to provide EPSDT services. *Westside Mothers v. Haverman,* 289 F. 3d 852 (6th Cir., 2002).

Early and Periodic Screening, Diagnostic, and Treatment Services 42 U.S.C. § 1396d(r)

The term "early and periodic screening, diagnostic, and treatment services" means the following items and services:

(1) **Screening services—**
    (A) which are provided—
        (i) at intervals which meet reasonable standards of medical and dental practice, as determined by the state after consultation with recognized medical and dental organizations involved in child health care and, with respect to immunizations under subparagraph (B)(iii), in accordance with the schedule referred to in section 1396s(c)(2)(B)(i) of this title for pediatric vaccines and
        (ii) at such other intervals indicated as medically necessary, to determine the existence of certain physical or mental illnesses or conditions; and
    (B) which shall at a minimum include—
        (i) a comprehensive health and developmental history (including assessment of both physical and mental health development),
        (ii) a comprehensive unclothed physical exam,
        (iii) appropriate immunizations (according to the schedule referred to in section 1396s(c)(2)(B)(i) of this title for pediatric vaccines) according to age and health history,
        (iv) laboratory tests (including lead blood level assessment appropriate for age and risk factors), and
        (v) health education (including anticipatory guidance).

(2) **Vision services—**

(A) which are provided—
  (i) at intervals which meet reasonable standards of medical practice, as determined by the state after consultation with recognized medical organizations involved in child health care, and
  (ii) at such other intervals, indicated as medically necessary, to determine the existence of a suspected illness or condition; and
(B) which shall at a minimum include diagnosis and treatment for defects in vision, including eyeglasses.

(3) **Dental services—**
(A) which are provided—
  (i) at intervals which meet reasonable standards of dental practice, as determined by the state after consultation with recognized dental organizations involved in child health care, and
  (ii) at such other intervals indicated as medically necessary, to determine the existence of a suspected illness or condition; and

(4) **Hearing services—**
(A) which are provided—
  (i) at intervals which meet reasonable standards of medical practice, as determined by the state after consultation with a recognized medical organizations involved in child health care, and
(B) which shall at a minimum include diagnosis and treatment for defects in hearing, including hearing aids.

(5) Such other necessary heath care, diagnostic services, treatment, and other measures described in subsection (a) of this section to correct or ameliorate defects and physical and mental illnesses and conditions discovered by the screening services, whether or not such services are covered under the state plan.

Nothing in this subchapter shall be construed as limiting providers of early and periodic screening, diagnostic, and treatment services to providers who are qualified to provide all of the items and services described in the previous sentence or as preventing a provider that is qualified under the plan to furnish one or more (but not all) of such items or services from being qualified to provide such items and services as part of early and periodic screening, diagnostic, and treatment services. The Secretary shall, not later than July 1, 1990, and every 12 months thereafter, develop and set annual participation goals for each state for participation of individuals who are covered under the state plan under this subchapter in early and periodic screening, diagnostic, and treatment services. (Emphasis added)

The sum total of health services offered to a child sometimes may require hunting through a variety of sources, such as the state's EPSDT program, Medicaid provisions generally, Maternal and Child Health Services Block Grant Program (Title V of the Social Security Act, 42 U.S.C. § 701 *et seq.*(1992); and the Women, Infants and Children Supplemental Food Program (WIC, Child Nutrition Act, 42 U.S.C. §1381-83(d) (1992). Services offered through other parts of the Medicaid program also are described in the federal law. A good way to start is to turn to a few articles where authors have done the search and compilation. Recommended is English, A., Morreale, M. & Stinnet, A. (1999) *Adolescents in Public Health Insurance Programs: Medicaid and CHIP,* published by the Center for Adolescent Health & the Law in Chapel Hill, North Carolina. Another useful source is the neglect-abuse chapter in REPRESENTING THE CHILD CLIENT (Lexis 2000), edited by Dale *et al.* Because the details of Medicaid laws change so frequently, it is important to ascertain the latest revisions of the law before bringing a disputed Medicaid issue before the court.

What kinds of problems will arise for advocates regarding the interpretation of Medicaid, EPSDT, and SCHIP laws? One problem is that not all of the laws' terms are defined. For example, in the EPSDT statute, the crucial term "medically necessary" that limits the treatment of medical conditions has never been fully defined. There are HHS regulations that interpret the statute, although not as helpfully as one could hope. For example, at 42 U.S.C. §1396a(a) the law states:

A state plan for medical assistance must—
    (10) provide—
        (B) that the medical assistance made available to any individual described in subparagraph (A)—
            (i) shall not be less in amount, duration, or scope than the medical assistance made available to any other such individual.

Interpreting that law, the HHS regulation at 42 C.F.R. §440.230 states:

(a) The plan must specify the amount, duration, and scope of each service that it provides for—
    (1) The categorically needy; and
    (2) Each covered group of medically needy.
(b) Each service must be sufficient in amount, duration, and scope to reasonably achieve its purpose
(c) The Medicaid agency may not arbitrarily deny or reduce the amount, duration, or scope of a required service under sections 440.210 and 440.220 to an otherwise eligible recipient solely because of the diagnosis, type of illness, or condition.

(d) The agency may place appropriate limits on a service based on such criteria as medical necessity or on utilization control procedures.

The EPSDT law provides for support services in addition to basic screening, diagnosis, and treatment. These often are overlooked because social workers and other advocates are concentrating on obtaining core medical services. Support services include transportation to appointments, and even case management to help set up appointments. 42 C.F.R. §62.

2. Funding

Most health services for children are received through a medical plan or program specifically designed for foster children, and administered by either the state's foster care agency, a health services agency, or a combination of both. A growing trend is for the public foster care agency to contract directly with service providers, often in a managed care format. Funds for health services are part federal and part state. The source of federal funds is found in Titles XVIII and XIX of the Social Security Act. The state contributes a percentage of the funds. In addition, for certain services the state may contribute discretionary funds it received as part of a federal block grant or even state-generated funds unconnected with the federal government.

The interweaving of funding streams for health services is complex, but in the common case there is no need to track the money back to its source. Usually Medicaid money is provided to the foster care agency through the state's health services agency, or it is given directly to the foster care agency, which manages it through contracts with service providers. Contracts tend to be of the "managed care" type, meaning that the provider offers a certain number of services to a certain number of people at a specified total cost to the contracting agency. In other words, payment is capped, and any services that exceed that cap must be absorbed by the provider or, if the service is mandated and the provider cannot cover the cost of it, by the foster care agency.

Problems arise when not all services a child needs are provided under the managed care contract, but are compensated instead on a "fee for service" basis—meaning that the child must be connected with a specialist who is outside the main provider's network and who will bill separately for services. Mental health services, drug treatment, and obstetrics and gynecology are examples of services that may not be included in the managed care contract. When a child needs services outside the main contract, the primary managed care provider may fail to connect the child to the fee-for-service providers, and the foster parent or social worker may not know how to make the connections either. It may fall to an advocate to explain to a court, agency, or even a service provider what the barriers are to obtaining services, and how to overcome them. Fee-for-service questions can sometimes be resolved by arranging a customized billing and remuneration plan. More often, they also involve finding the right expert, making appointments, and transporting the child to an office outside of the usual clinic. In this instance, it may be helpful to draw upon the Medicaid services for case management and transportation. 42 C.F.R. §62.

For attorneys and administrators who often must deal with funding issues, it may be helpful to keep a copy of the state's Medicaid plan for foster care children at hand, as well as a copy of the foster care or health agency's contracts with medical service providers. The state's plan is filed with the U.S. Department of Health and Human Services. The plan and contracts should also be available through the state agency that manages foster care or health services.

In the area of reproductive health, there is one medical service often requested that federal Medicaid usually will not cover: abortion. Unless the mother's life is at risk, or the pregnancy has been caused by rape or incest, only state funds may be used to pay for abortions. P.L. 105-78, §§509, 510 (1997). Some states do pay for abortions through their Medicaid programs, drawing only on state funds. When a teenager requests abortion services, once the issue of funding is decided, there are additional legal issues that must be sorted out. Do state laws require parental notification or parental consent? If so, is it possible and appropriate to petition for judicial bypass? Is there a mature minors doctrine? The U.S. Supreme Court determined in 1979 in *Bellotti v. Baird,*443 U.S. 622, that there could be no laws that absolutely prohibit abortions for a whole class of women, in this case minors. *Bellotti* set up criteria for state statutes: the pregnant teen must be permitted to show that she is mature and well informed, or that an abortion would be in her best interests. She must be granted anonymity and the case must proceed swiftly enough for her to actually obtain the abortion if permission is granted. Gradually those state supreme courts that have sustained parental consent or notification laws have required them to contain due process procedures, like the opportunity to be represented by counsel when judicial bypass petitions are before the court. Some states have rejected parental consent and notification requirements as violating their state's constitutional guarantee of privacy. E.g. *American Academy of Pediatrics v. Lundgren,* 940 P.2d 797 (CA. 1997); and *In re T.W.,* 551 So.2d 1186 (Fl. 1989).

Teens may acquire other kinds of reproductive care, like pregnancy counseling and treatment for sexually transmitted diseases without parental (or foster care agency) notification or consent. Other than for abortions, Medicaid funding is available for the whole range of reproductive services, from contraceptive counseling and prenatal care to post-natal care.[3]

Children with severe impairments may qualify for Supplemental Security Income (SSI). The Personal Responsibility and Work Opportunity Reconciliation Act of 1996, P.L.104-725, tightened the rules for funding children with disabilities who qualified under Title XVI of the SSA, §1381 *et seq.* The eligibility criteria now is more difficult to meet than in the days before the mid-1990's, when almost all foster children were considered to have "maladaptive behavior." The Act eliminates the term "maladaptive behavior" as a diagnosis (though it can be considered as a symptom of an illness or one element of a DSM-IV-R diagnosis). The current eligibility standard is:

> An individual under the age of 18 shall be considered disabled for the purposes of this title if that individual has a medically determinable physical or mental impairment, which results in marked and severe functional limitations, and which can be expected to result in death or which has lasted or can be expected to last for a continuous period of not less than 12 months. [§211 of the Act; 42 U.S.C. §1382c(a)(3)(C)(i)]

All cases current at the time of the Act were required to be reevaluated. Many children were dropped from the SSI rolls because they could not prove that their mental or behavioral impairment had a medical basis. The Social Security Administration is required to review the case of every child SSI recipient at least once every three years.

The procedures under SSI to initially qualify a child for funds, and then to periodically review the qualifications, are complex. There are three main federal legal references: Title XVI, 42 U.S.C. §§1381 *et seq;* federal regulations at 20 C.F.R., especially Sections 404 and 416; and the Social Security Administration's Program Operations Manual System (POMS).

The questions of who shall shepherd children through the complex eligibility and redetermination processes, and who shall receive and manage the SSI funds often are settled by identifying the "representative payee." The Social Security Agency appears to reserve to itself the decision about who (or what organization) the representative payee shall be in any particular case. 20 C.F.R. §416.601. The foster care agency is the usual representative payee for foster children, though foster parents or kin can be so designated. The regulations do not preclude teenagers from managing the funds if they have proved themselves mature or are about to age out of the system. 20 C.F.R. §416.610(b). One theme that has run through SSI litigation is whether it is fair for a foster agency to use a child's SSI funds to compensate the state for its costs to support the child. The U.S. Supreme Court has now settled that issue in favor of the foster care agency, *Washington State Department of Social and Health Services v. Estate of Danny Keffeler, et al.,* 537 U.S. 371 (2003).

An Agency may apply for both Title IV-E funds and SSI funds for a foster child, but the Title IV-E funds will then be reduced by the amount of the SSI funds. SSA sec. 402(a)(24); 406(a); 407; 472(a); 473(a); SSI Program Operations Manual System Part 5, Supplemental Security Income Chapter 008-Income, Subchapter 30-Unearned Income. See Children's Bureau Policy 8.4D. What then is the benefit of applying for SSI? The services for which SSI qualifies a child can be important, even crucial. Some state agencies have a separate office to assess a child's SSI eligibility and guide the case through the process, while other agencies assign that task to the child's main social worker.

In addition to children who qualify for SSI through Title VI of the SSA, some children will receive SSI survivor benefits through Title II, 42 USC sec. 401 *et seq.* These are social security benefits from the estate of a dead parent. There are fewer legal issues arising in this population once the representative payee is selected.

3. Standards

Sometimes an issue before the court is whether the provider has offered or given services of sufficient quality. How does one determine the quality of medical services? The standard may be described in the law or regulation itself. For example, the EPSDT law specifically states the categories of services that must be offered (vision, hearing, dental, mental health, etc.), and requires a diagnosis to be made, and mandates follow-up treatment. Screenings for medical problems are to be routine, although the law leaves it to professional groups to determine what is a sufficient routine. The Child Welfare League of America (CWLA) has taken a close look at the particular health needs of foster children. In its *Checklist of Needed Services for Children in Foster Care,* found in its book MAKING MANAGED HEALTH CARE WORK FOR KIDS IN FOSTER CARE, as well as at www.cwla.org/programs/health/checklist.htm, CWLA addresses sufficient medical care for this population.

Child Welfare League of America Checklist of Needed Services for Children in Foster Care

☐ Immediate eligibility for services

☐ 7 day/week, 24 hour/day availability of emergency services

☐ Community-based services

☐ Culturally competent services (including language capacity that reflects consumer's primary language)

- [ ] Initial health screening appropriate to the child's circumstances and agency concerns at the time the child enters foster care (within 24 hours)
- [ ] Comprehensive, multidisciplinary health, mental health and developmental assessment within one month of child's placement
- [ ] Screening tests for common medical conditions such as anemia, lead poisoning, etc. and risk assessments and screening tests for specialized conditions including HIV and in utero drug exposure if indicated
- [ ] Developmental and mental health evaluations on a regular schedule
- [ ] Immunizations
- [ ] Comprehensive dental services including relief of pain and infection, restoration of teeth, and maintenance of dental health
- [ ] Follow-up diagnostic and treatment services for all conditions and problems identified in the health assessment and developmental and mental health evaluations
- [ ] Covered costs of hearing aids, eyeglasses, and other equipment
- [ ] Ongoing primary and preventive health care services including reassessments at a minimum every 6 months
- [ ] Access to appropriate specialty and subspecialty care
- [ ] Case management designating one individual or center to be responsible for coordinating all aspects of the health care of foster children including a plan to meet the child's health care needs and identification of responsibilities and recommendations for follow-up care. Case management services must include assistance with scheduling appointments and transportation
- [ ] Coordinated medical and psychosocial recordkeeping

The U.S. Maternal and Child Health Bureau addresses preventive medical services for children of all ages and socioeconomic groups in a very readable document called *Bright Futures: Guidelines for Health Supervision of Infants, Children and Adolescents,*edited by Morris Green, M.D. That population also is the subject of *Guidelines for Health Supervision III,* edited by M. Stein, which is directed to pediatric physicians. The American Medical Association has focused on adolescent health care in its *Guidelines for Adolescent Preventive Services* (GAPS), edited by Arthur B. Elster, M.D. and Naomi J. Zuznets, Ph.D. *GAPS* helpfully addresses many of the issues faced by foster teens, such as sexually transmitted diseases, special education, and diet.

Note that the Washington Supreme Court, in a class action suit against the state's foster care system, has called such standards "aspirational" and not admissible as evidence of accepted professional judgement. *Braam ex rel. Braam*

v. *State*, 81 P.3d 851 (Wash. 2003). Another state court could reach a different conclusion.

Another resource for advocates who need to pursue the issue of adequate quality in the delivery of health care may be the state's contract with health service providers, to the extent that it addresses standards for medical care. Many states, however, do not have contracts that reach a desirable degree of specificity.

State foster care agencies under consent decrees from a class action suit or affected by consent decrees against another state agency may have specific standards imposed by a federal court. For example, in Missouri the foster care agency is required by *G.L. v Stangler*, 873 F. Supp. 252 (W.D.Mo.1994) to meet described standards that conform to the federal EPSDT law. In the District of Columbia, EPSDT standards that address such factors as government outreach, transportation, and thoroughness affect foster care health services even though the suit addresses all Medicaid populations, *Salazar v. District of Columbia*, 954 F. Supp. 278(1996), CA 93-452 (GK), 1997 WL 3006876, reprinted in Medicare and Medicaid Guide Para. 45, 189 (D. D.C. 1/17/97 (remedial order)).

D. Access to Special Education

Under federal law all children have a right to a "free and appropriate public education" in the "least restrictive environment" available. The Individuals with Disabilities Education Act (IDEA), P.L. 94-142 (1975), as amended (1990), 20 U.S.C. §§ 1400 *et seq*. This important provision assures that children with special educational needs will be evaluated and given additional services that provide a "reasonable opportunity to learn." *Board of Education of Hendrick Hudson School District v. Rowley*, 458 U.S. 176 (1982). Many experts believe that every child who enters foster care should be evaluated for special education services. Eligibility for these services can be raised at school, or as part of the EPSDT exam when problems are discovered in areas like mental health, hearing, and vision.

The processes by which these services are selected are described in federal law at 20 U.S.C. §1414 and in the regulations at 34 C.F.R. §§ 300 *et seq*. State laws implement, and sometimes extend or interpret, the federal mandates. Generally the child receives an initial evaluation of education performance using "a variety of assessment tools and strategies to gather functional and developmental information." 20 U.S.C. §1414(b). Based on evaluation results, if special education is found to be necessary, an Individual Education Plan (IEP) is developed that describes in great detail the problems and remedial services required to resolve them. The IEP is reviewed annually with adjustments made when the situation has changed. Legal issues can arise throughout the process. For example:

- Who shall give the required consent for evaluation when the child is in foster care?
- Are the assessment and evaluation tools the right ones to reveal the child's problems?
- While the child is in foster care, do the biological parents have residual parental rights that extend to education?
- Who shall be the "surrogate parent" to participate on the IEP team if the biological parents are not available?
- Does the IEP describe the correct services?
- Should the child be placed in a private school or is a public school the "least restrictive environment"?
- Should assessments, evaluations, and services arising from physical or mental impairments be compensated through Medicaid rather than IDEA?

Tensions between parents, the education system, and the foster care system exist at nearly every point. There is an administrative appeals process which usually must be exhausted before court action occurs. To further complicate matters, some service issues will arise under Section 504 of *The Rehabilitation Act*, 29 U.S.C. §794 (1973), particularly if the disability is one that "substantially limits one or more major life activities." 34 C.F.R. § 104.3(j). If the court enters the fray at this point and orders specific services, such as educational placement in a particular school, legal issues may arise relating to whether state law gives the court is acting within its authority.

E. Placement with Siblings

An unfortunate but common consequence of the foster care system is that biological families become fragmented. Brothers and sisters end up in different foster homes, adopted by different families. Some siblings return home while others remain in foster care. An issue that has drawn some attention over the years has been the need to keep siblings together. Even if siblings cannot be placed or adopted together, what steps can or must be taken to assure that siblings can continue to visit with one another or at least know one another's whereabouts?

There are two aspects to this. One is the social aspect—that is, focusing only on the social needs of the children, what would be best for them? The second is the legal aspect—what legal rights, if any, do siblings have to maintain a relationship or to be placed together? The first issue is addressed case-by-case. The law is flexible enough for a judge to mandate continued sibling contact or placement together if this is in the child's best interests. However, the existence of a legal right to sibling association with one another is far harder to find. Some states have enacted laws addressing sibling rights. For example, a Maryland statute reads:

Md. Code Ann., Fam. Law. §5-525.2 Sibling Visitation Rights
   (a) *Petition for visitation rights*—Any siblings who are separated due to a foster care or adoptive placement may petition a court, including a juvenile court with jurisdiction over one or more of the siblings, for reasonable sibling visitation rights.
   (b) *Role of court*—If a petitioner under this section petitions a court to issue a visitation decree or to amend an order, the court:
      (1) may hold a hearing to determine whether visitation is in the best interest of the children;
      (2) shall weigh the relative interests of each child and base its decision on the best interests of the children promoting the greatest welfare and lease harm to the children; and
      (3) may issue an appropriate order or degree.

Indeed, in a post-adoption case, one court found that "siblings possess the natural, inherent and inalienable right to visit with each other." *L.K.C.B. and H.L.K. v. G. and H.,* 497 A. 2d 215 (N.J. Super.Ct. Ch.Div. 1985). Nonetheless, the small but growing body of case law reveals that courts refuse to recognize a U.S. Constitutional right to sibling association. It is worth noting that the U.S. Supreme Court declined an opportunity to address the issue. *Adoption of Hugo,* 700 N.E. 2d 516 (Mass. 1998) (Biological siblings' relationship not entitled to "presumptive weight") *cert. denied* 526 U.S. 1034 (1999). Despite lack of recognition for a constitutional right of sibling association, state legislatures and state courts would not be precluded from enacting and recognizing such a right.

F. "Aging Out" and Independent Living

What are the legal issues that affect extending benefits to youth who have reached an age of majority but who remain in the neglect abuse system after the usual date for "aging out"? The federal definition of foster care is:

> …24-hour substitute care for children placed away from their parents or guardians and for whom the state agency has placement and care responsibility. [45 C.F.R. §1355.20]

Title IV-E foster care funds potentially are available until a child's 19th birthday, at which point they cease. The legal basis for this, according to 42 U.S.C.

§ 672 (a), is that a child qualifies for the foster care maintenance program if he or she is a "dependent child" as described in 42 U.S.C. § 606(a):

> The term "dependent child" means a needy child...(2) who is (A) under the age of eighteen, or (B) at the option of the state, under the age of nineteen and a full-time student in a secondary school (or in the equivalent level of vocational or technical training), if, before he attains age nineteen, he may reasonably be expected to complete the program of such secondary school (or training).

Any extensions beyond age nineteen must be funded from other sources.

The three main models for extending care beyond the date of a youth's majority are (1) by statutory law, which sometimes contains criteria for the extension; (2) by foster care agency's decision, often involving a contract offered to selected youth; and (3) by a court's assertion of judicial authority to extend jurisdiction. In addition, some states by statute set twenty-one as the upper limit for benefits, beyond which there is no extension.

A great leap forward in extension of benefits to youth who would have aged out at their majority occurred when Congress passed The Foster Care Independence Act of 1999, P.L.106-169; 113 Stat 1822 (1999). (This Act replaces the former Independent Living Initiative.) Funds distributed through Section 477 of the Social Security Act are allotted to each state according to its needs and plans for utilization as submitted to the U.S. Department of Health and Human Services. Plans could contain any mix of benefits, including complete support in independent living units, extension of Medicaid, tuition waivers, and job training. At a minimum, the benefits are available to selected youth who are in the system at age nineteen, although the state could include more youth, for example by lowering the age to sixteen. The Act was passed in a time of budget surpluses and is being implemented in a time of budget shortfalls, so in many states there are fewer benefits to be distributed than Congress envisioned.

The legal issues that may arise include (1) whether jurisdiction was properly extended under state law; (2) whether a youth was properly selected or wrongly eliminated from extension of benefits; (3) whether the youth was fully informed of responsibilities under the Act and voluntarily accepted the extension of jurisdiction; and (4) whether promised benefits in fact occurred.

G. Protection Against Harm

Do foster children have a right to be safe in their placements? *Deshaney v. Winnebago County Social Services Department*, 489 U.S. 189 (1989), excludes

action against a state agency by children who are not in the agency's legal custody (that is, not in foster care) even when the agency has opened a social service case for them because it is aware the children are at risk for abuse or neglect. Although the U.S. Supreme Court has not decided whether foster
children have a right to protection (the distinction being that such children
actually are in state's legal custody), the Second Circuit's *Doe* case established
that children have a cause of action against the public and private foster care
agencies for failure to properly supervise children and for injuries inflicted on
foster children while in foster homes. *Doe v. N.Y. City Dep't of Social Ser-*
*vices,*649 F.2d 134 (2d Cir. 1981). At this time it seems safe to say, even in the
wake of *Deshaney,* that foster children have a cause of action against the foster care agency if they are injured in the foster home by their foster parents or
because of the negligence of the foster family.

H. Privacy

Questions relating to whether children have rights to privacy cannot be answered simply. Children do have some privacy rights, but they are not coex-
tensive with the rights claimed by adults. While the potential for privacy exists in many aspects of a child's life, it is influenced by such factors as the age
of the child and how vital the issue is to the foster child's legal case. For some
purposes, such as privacy about abortion, a foster teenager's rights are almost
identical to those of an adult woman, differing only when the teen is subject
to state-enacted parental notification or consent laws. On the other hand,
school records are open to examination by parents as a matter of federal law,
Family Educational Rights and Privacy Act (FERPA), 20 U.S.C. §1232g, and
it could be difficult to close them to parents in a neglect-abuse proceeding
even where custody has shifted to the foster care agency, absent a court order.

It is not uncommon for a child outside the foster care system to be able to
control access to mental health and substance abuse treatment records if the
child initiated treatment without parental consent. But by federal law a court
can determine that there is "good cause" to receive the treatment records, and
that is the action likely to be taken in a neglect-abuse case. 42 U.S.C. § 290dd-
2, C.F.R. §§2.31, 2.61, 2.63, 2.64. As to infectious diseases such as HIV, many
states have statutes that permit the judge to find that physician-patient privilege does not apply to a child in a neglect-abuse case. E.g. D.C. Code §4-
1321.05.

The privacy rights of foster children, as a subgroup of children-in-general,
have not gotten much attention and there is little material that could serve as
a useful guide. In most situations, it would appear that foster children should

be no different than any other children and would have whatever privacy rights were available to children generally. As a practical matter, though, foster care agencies have the same access to a foster child's records and pertinent information that the parents have. The description of persons who are entitled to "all records" in a neglect-abuse case, according to the Child Abuse Prevention and Treatment Act,(CAPTA) 42 U.S.C. §5106a(b)(2)(A)(v) is very broad. Basically the group includes every government agency that has need for the information in order to protect children and carry out their responsibilities, and a number of other non-governmental groups. A child advocate could argue for a protective order and, if granted, that might limit the number of people who could examine the records. Even if it could be argued that a foster child could completely prohibit disclosure of records to the agency, using as precedent that a child outside the system could prohibit disclosure to parents, in the dynamics of the courtroom, foster children do not find much support for privacy. The agency and the judge want to acquire as much information about the child as possible, and it would take a vigorous child advocate with some inventive arguments to prevail against that inquiry.

I. Right of Native American Children to Tribal Supervision

The Indian Child Welfare Act of 1978 (ICWA), P.L. 95-608, 92 Stat 3069, 25 U.S.C. §§ 1901-1963, permits a Native American tribe to intervene at any point in a proceeding that removes a Native American child from a Native American parent, and to shift that proceeding to a tribal court. This power is broad and should not be underestimated. The parent may not be living on the reservation, the child may never have visited tribal lands, the mother may not be a tribal member, and the Native American father may have consented to the proceeding in a state court, as in the case of *Mississippi Band of Choctaw Indians v. Holyfield*, 490 U.S. 30 (1989). Nevertheless, the tribe has the right to undo a state proceeding at any point, even after adoption. This legal regime is the only one in which a child (as well as the child's parent, Native American custodian, and tribe) may be the petitioner for removal of the case (§ 104). In effect, it establishes reciprocal rights: the right of the child to be raised in the tribe and the right of the tribe to claim its children.

In any foster care proceeding, as soon as it is discovered that the child has the tribal ties that the ICWA specifies, a registered letter must be sent to both the tribe and the Native American parent or custodian informing them of the action. Due process includes adequate notice and time to prepare a case, appointment of counsel if the parent or tribe cannot pay, and the high standard of clear and convincing evidence for any foster care placement outside the tribe. The tribe may decline to intervene once contacted, but a Native American parent or custodian may still withdraw consent to the foster care placement at any time, requiring the child to be returned to tribal jurisdiction. (§103(b)).

III. Conclusion

Certain federal laws contain important rights for foster children, for example the right to comprehensive health care (Medicaid, EPSDT), to a free and appropriate education (IDEA), and to a speedy permanent home after separation from the biological parents (ASFA). Because young children do not know about these rights and lack the skill to claim them, the rights will lie buried unless an advocate steps forward as an agent for the child. While CAPTA standards recommend that the advocate be a child's attorney, a guardian *ad litem, or* Court Appointed Special Advocate (CASA), in fact any interested adult could fill that crucial role, including a social worker, the judge, the government attorney, or a parent or relative. There is a great deal of literature that shows the shocking condition of foster children who could not obtain even the simplest treatment for the most pressing needs. Many children leave foster care in as terrible a condition as when they entered it. [4]

Children have no legally protected right to weigh in on the subject of whether they shall be raised by their biological parents, by relatives, or adopted by strangers. Yet again, conscientious representation can give them a voice. Both attorneys and guardians *ad litem* are required by professional standards of practice to consult children, taking into consideration their age, and to make their wishes known. In the end, it is *only* through adult representation that a child becomes visible to the other parties in her own case.

2

FOSTER PARENTS

CHAPTER GUIDE

I. Overview

A. Who are Foster Parents?

The terms "foster care", "foster child" and "foster parent" can each have two very different meanings. There is the foster care provided by operation of the modern child welfare system. This foster care results from the duty and the authority of the state to remove children from their family homes when conditions are unsafe and to continue to provide care for them in a family-like environment. This situation requires the state to create foster homes for children.

There is also "informal" foster care that occurs when one person (sometimes a family member) cares for the child of another. This arrangement is outside the formal state child welfare system, the parent does not receive payment from a government or agency, and the person has no ties to an agency.

Caretakers can be referred to as "foster parents" and the "foster child" can be considered to be in "foster care." This kind of foster care has been around for quite some time.

For our purposes the term foster care means the kind of foster care provided to children by the child welfare system. This kind of foster care involves foster parents who are recruited, trained, and licensed by the state (or private agency) and who care for children under the supervision of an agency and court system. Foster parents have some sort of formal agreement with the agency and their relationship with the child is created and defined by the legal system. Foster parents have been described as "individuals...who are not the lawful parents of the child, but merely act in a parental capacity because of a temporary contractual agreement with the state...." *Kerins v. Lima,* 680 N.E. 2d 32, 34 (Mass. 1997). Foster parents act as adult supervisors and provide safety, meals, and shelter and, unlike biological parents, they are reimbursed for their expenses in caring for the foster child. For legal descriptions of the differences between foster and biological parents, see *Andrews v. Otsego County,* 446 N.Y.S.2d 169 (Sup. Ct. 1982) and *Kerins v. Lima,* 680 N.E. 2d 32 (Mass. 1997).

Foster parents assume substantial responsibility and obligations when caring for foster children. They enter into a relationship with a government child welfare agency or a private foster care agency. They also have a relationship with the foster child. These obligations and relationships create many legal issues. Such issues include a foster parent's liability for injuries to and by foster children, a foster parent's procedural rights to participate in judicial and other proceedings involving foster children, and a foster parent's right to prevent removal of the foster children in their care and to maintain their relationship to (or to adopt) the foster child.

B. Foster Parents' Relationship to the Agency

The foster care agency, either a public agency or private agency under contract to the public agency, recruits, trains, and certifies or licenses foster parents. The agency has the responsibility to "place" the child into a foster home. The agency will try to ensure that the home selected will be able to care for the particular child placed into that home. The agency's social workers will supervise the placement by visiting the child in the home and at school, speaking to those familiar with the child, and reviewing information about the child.

The foster parent will have a formal, legal relationship with the agency that provides foster care and is responsible for the safety and welfare of the foster child. Usually this relationship will be contained in a formal written agreement with a public or private agency. This agreement will determine many of the most important aspects of the relationship, such as the duties and responsibilities of the foster parent and the agency, the role of the foster parents regarding planning for the child, reunification, and removal of the child and permanency. In addition to the agreement or contract, there are agency policies and practices that affect foster care. Often times, instead of an agreement, the agency will have the foster parents acknowledge that they have read and will abide by the agency's rules and policies.

One very important aspect of the foster parent-foster care agency relationship is its legal status. That is, are the foster parents independent contractors, employees of the agency, or something else? There is no easy answer to this question which will be further discussed later in this Chapter. The answer is determined either by state law, or by the actual agreement or contract, or by assessing the facts pertaining to the specific relationship at issue. If state law is unclear, the answer cannot be predicted and a court may eventually make this determination in the context of a lawsuit.

There are those who believe that foster parents ought to have some ability to preserve their relationship with the child in their care even when the agency recommends that the child ought to be removed. For instance, the foster parents may argue that the child should remain with them in foster care or that they should be allowed to adopt or obtain custody or guardianship of the child. However, the legal system has been slow to create enforceable rights for foster parents that would assure that their decisions and preferences regarding the care and treatment of the child be taken equally into account with the child's, biological parents' and the agency's preferences. Indeed, the legal system generally has not been hospitable to the argument that foster parents ought to have such rights. As of now foster parent's rights are for the most part limited to procedural matters. For example, if a child is going to be removed the foster parent may be entitled to advance notice and an opportunity to be heard on the merits of the removal. Even if foster parents are permitted to address the effect of the removal on the child — for instance, by asking whether the removal is in the best interest of the child —the law is very unclear as to the rights of the foster parent (or child) to actually prevent removal.

Foster parent status is never permanent. Usually certification must be renewed periodically and agencies can, under certain conditions, revoke certification. Moreover, no one can be forced to be a foster parent nor can a foster parent be forced to keep foster children in their home. Foster parents can cease to be foster parents by simply informing the agency that they no longer wish to care for foster children and the children would be removed. The agency can terminate the foster parents' status and remove the child at a moment's notice. Even if the foster parent's status was unchanged and they wished to remain foster parents, the agency can simply remove children. States normally require prior notice of such removals and allow the removal to be challenged either administratively or in court. In addition, states usually have an administrative review process that allows foster parents to challenge a denial of an application to be a foster parent or to challenge the termination of their status as foster parents (revocation of certification or refusal to renew). Such a process is designed to prevent agencies from acting arbitrarily and capriciously or for illegal reasons. (For example, see Maryland's administrative hearing process at Title 7 Code of Maryland Regulations (COMAR) Subtitle 1 Chapter 4, Administrative Hearings).

Traditionally, foster parents were volunteers and received no direct compensation for their services. Instead, foster parents received money to feed and clothe the children and to reimburse them for the added expenses of caring for another person in the household. This tradition is rapidly changing. In addition to providing funds that are intended to reimburse the foster parent for the costs of caring for a child there are now are foster care agencies that pay foster parents for their services. It is thought that payment can enable the recruitment and retention of high quality caregivers. Indeed, there can even be "full-time foster parents" whose occupation is the care of special needs or high maintenance children.

There are also "kinship foster parents." These foster parents are biologically or legally related to the child. Kinship foster parents are not traditional foster parents but their status is usually created by statutes, regulations, and practices. Sometimes the training and certification requirements differ from those imposed on other foster parents (such as unrelated foster parents) and sometimes kinship care providers do not receive any compensation at all for the care they provide.

In conclusion, the foster parent-foster care agency relationship is governed by statutes, regulation, contract, and by the practices and procedures of the agency. There are very few cases that address the legal aspects of being a foster parent. Because of the paucity of the cases and the significant variation in state laws and factual circumstances in these cases, it is not entirely accurate to say that there exists "foster parent law." When courts do address the foster parent- agency relationship they usually have done so by focusing on a particular aspect of the relationship—liability, preference in adopting, right to participate in court matters, due process, and right to prevent removal. Indeed, when it comes to "foster parent law" there are no broad generalizations to be made that would be true in all circumstances. For example, as is explained in greater detail later in Appendix A, whether or not foster parents are liable for the acts of foster children varies widely from state to state and can be affected by the precise circumstances at issue.

C. Foster Parents' Relationship with the Foster Child

The foster parent-child relationship can be characterized as someone acting as a parent to a child as a result of a "temporary contractual agreement." By contrast, a biological parent-child relationship is "not contractual, it is familial." *Kerins v. Lima,* 680 N.E. 2d 32, 34 (Mass. 1997).

Foster parents do not have a formal legal relationship with the child in the same way that they have a formal legal relationship with the foster care agency. There is very little law on the legal relationship between the foster parent and the foster child. Foster parents have physical custody of the child. In most cases they do not have a formal legal relationship such as legal custody of, or guardianship, over the child. It is the (public) agency that has legal custody of the child. Thus, foster parents do not stand in the same role as legal custodians and guardians and cannot exert the kind of control such caretakers have. The most accurate way to characterize the foster parent-child relationship would be by reference to the obligations and responsibilities of the foster parent to the child and by reference to the limitations imposed on the foster parents' decision-making discretion. In any event, the legal relationship would be derivative of, and determined by, the foster parent's relationship with the agency that placed the child and would be affected by the extent of the foster parent's authority over the child. There almost always is a formal written agreement that requires the foster parent to care for a child who will be placed into the foster home under the authority granted to the agency. The foster parent assumes a legal duty to provide care in accordance with applicable laws and regulations and also becomes accountable to the agency and the court. (There can be, especially for older children, a "contract" between the child and the foster parents which would spell out the obligations and responsibilities and consequences of the child's misbehavior or failure to follow rules. These are not binding legal contracts. They are in the nature of "house rules" or an understanding between the foster parents and foster child.)

Traditionally, the role of foster parents has been limited to providing food, clothing, shelter, transportation and, in general, caring for the child's daily needs. Foster parents have been asked to provide transportation for the child, and schedule routine medical and dental appointments. Foster parents have been charged with properly spending the money provided to them by the agency, but have had no independent financial obligation to their foster children. Foster parents have been expected to provide discipline but with limited authority. All other issues typically have been referred to the social worker. No matter what the role and no matter what the legal relationship, foster parents had, and continue to have, a duty to properly care for and be attentive to the needs of the foster child.

The role of foster parents is changing. In the past, there were only "traditional foster parents" like the ones described above. Nowadays foster parents, including "traditional foster parents," might be part of a "treatment team" that addresses the needs of the foster child. The opinions and insights of the foster parents will be considered in planning and the foster parent may attend clinical staffings and administrative reviews. This expansion of the foster parents' role especially pertains to those foster parents caring for special needs children. Referred to by such terms as "treatment foster parents" or "therapeutic foster homes," these foster parents undertake many of the responsibilities of social workers when making decisions and planning for the child. Usually such decisions and plans would be reviewed and ratified at some point by the agency social worker and her supervisors.

It is possible to envision a foster care system in which foster parents are able to exercise some of the authority that is normally thought of as "legal custody," similar to when a grandparent gets legal custody of a grandchild. This expanded authority could impose upon foster parents a financial responsibility they currently do not have. However, such status conflicts with the responsibility of the agency and the authority of the court. Remember, the child is in foster care only because the state had the legal authority to remove the child from the family, and the legal system, through the court, has the responsibility to ensure the child's safety and well being. Thus, the tension and conflict between foster parents on the one hand, and agencies and courts on the other, is built into the system by design if not by necessity. The foster parent has responsibility to care for the child, but not unilateral authority to make those decisions made by legal custodians. By contrast, the court or the agency has the legal authority to make decisions, but delegates to the foster parents the day-to-day obligation to care for the child.

D. Foster Parents as Advocates for Children

In the past, foster parents were caretakers who provided day-to-day care for children and carried out tasks as directed by the agency. Although there is little doubt that foster parents occupy a most critical place in the child welfare system, the contributions of foster parents have been minimized or even intentionally ignored. Consequently, foster parents have formed local and national organizations (for example, The National Foster Parent Association, www.nfpainc.org) to enhance their visibility and their relationship with foster care agencies and the government.

Most foster parents view themselves as more than mere "care providers" and consider themselves to be advocates and protectors for the children placed into their care. On the other hand, and as much as agencies view foster parents as reliable and conscientious advocates, agencies are also sensitive to any reduction in their authority at the hands of foster parents. In response to both of these considerations and to insure that foster parents can properly effectuate their role and be advocates for foster children, some states have enacted laws that specify the "rights" of foster parents. For instance, Tennessee has a "foster parent's rights" statute that enhances the ability of the foster parents to obtain information about the foster child and to influence decisions regarding the care and treatment of the child. (Tenn. Code Ann. § 37-2-415 (2003)).[5]

II. Significant Legal Issues

A. Authority of Foster Parents

Nothing is more confusing or contentious than the division of authority between and among the foster parents, agency social worker, biological parents, and the court. Affecting this authority are laws, regulations, and agency practices which differ widely from state to state. As a general rule the authority of foster parents is derived from and subject to the custodial authority of the agency. E.g. *Adoption of a Minor,* 438 N.E. 2d 138 (1982); *In the Interest of Hastings,* 318 N.W. 2d 80 (1982) (Foster care is temporary, designed to provide for a child until a permanent home can be located); *In the Interest of R.K.W.,* 689 S.W. 2d 647 (Mo. App. 1985) (Agency had legal custody, foster parents have physical custody). Foster parents can be given specific authority to act on behalf of the child. For example, Colorado allows (but does not require) foster parents to assume liability for a minor in their care who is applying for a driver's license. Colorado Rev. Stat. Ann §42-2-108.

There is little doubt that foster parents can and must exercise some authority over the foster child in their homes. Traditionally this authority has been restricted to the day-to-day decisions pertaining to the basic needs of the child. Most, if not all other decisions, would be referred to the agency social worker. The most important exercise of authority would involve discipline and in this area the discretion of the foster parents would be limited by regulation and agency practices. The agency can place restraints on discipline by encouraging some forms and discouraging or even prohibiting others. For instance, foster parents are usually prohibited from utilizing any form of corporal punishment. Maryland's foster home regulations state that "a foster parent may not [a]llow the [foster] child to be disciplined by (a) Corporal punishment; (b) Deprivation of food, clothing, shelter, care, or emotional support; (c) Physical restraint; (d) Isolation; or (e) Demeaning verbal abuse. Title 7 Code of Maryland Regulations (COMAR) .05.02.09.C. 10. Many other states have statutes or regulations similar to Maryland's.

Foster parents have little real authority regarding medical care. Their role is usually confined to taking the child to regular checkups, or monitoring health and alerting the social worker when the need for intervention occurs. Obviously, foster parents can bring children for emergency care but cannot usually authorize treatment. The agency social worker (or the court) would be responsible for such matters as hospital treatment, other than routine checkups, school enrollment and educational issues, and mental health treatment.

Foster parents have limited authority regarding education. Foster parents usually do not have authority to enroll children in school without agency permission. Foster children are usually enrolled in the public school which they would attend if they were the biological children of the foster parents or enrolled in a special education program. (There is no legal reason why foster children cannot attend private school to be paid by the agency, although as a practical matter foster children almost always attend public school unless they are special needs children). The responsibilities and obligations for monitoring school progress and education-related activities are divided between social workers and foster parents. A trend has been to delegate certain responsibilities and authority to foster parents. For instance, the foster parents and not the social worker might attend parent-student meetings and report to the social worker any major issues that need to be addressed. Foster parents can be surrogate parents for special education purposes. 34 C.F.R. §300.20(b), 20 U.S.C. §1401(19); 34 C.F.R. §300.515, 20 U.S.C. §1415(b)(2).

While it is expected that foster parents will allow foster children to accompany them to church or religious activities, foster parents cannot change a child's religious orientation. Whether or not an agency will change a child's foster care placement based on the biological parent's complaint that the child is being exposed to religious beliefs unacceptable to the parent can be an issue. *Walker v. Johnson*, 891 F. Supp 1040 (M.D. Pa. 1995) (Not in the best interest of children to change foster care arrangement even if failure to do so would result in them not receiving instruction in the religion of the biological mother's choice). (This issue is discussed in Chapter Three, II. B. Biological Parents.)

Foster parents are subject to child abuse and neglect laws just like biological parents. There are unfortunately foster parents who do abuse or neglect foster children in their care. Foster parents must also confront the possibility that they will be unjustly accused of mistreating a foster child. When foster parents are accused they can find themselves having to refute the allegations. They can also be placed on registry of abusive/neglectful parents, or even face criminal charges. Recently some agencies have started providing training to foster parents designed to minimize the possibility that they will be falsely accused of child maltreatment. Such training includes monitoring, supervision, identifying behaviors associated with past maltreatment, responding to the child's threats that allegations of maltreatment will be made, and "left-alone" situations.

B. Liability of Foster Parents

If a foster child is injured or mistreated or if a foster child injures someone or destroys property it is possible that the foster parents or the agency will be held legally responsible and will be sued. Therefore, foster parents and agencies do need to be constantly vigilant to circumstances that can result in liability. It is not being overly cautious to conclude that anything generating an "unusual incident report" would need to be examined for potential liability, especially situations involving lack of diligence on the part of a foster parent, injury or suspected injury to a foster child, or injury or damage caused by a foster child. Foster parent liability issues are addressed in detail in Appendix A.

C. Standards for Foster Care

Foster care is regulated by a network of statutory and regulatory schemes and best practices. The Child Welfare League of America, the National Association of Social Workers, and other organizations have extensive compilations of standards that apply to foster parenting and foster care. Training and monitoring foster parents are usually regulated in considerable detail. A state can by statute or regulation impose these standards and practices on agencies or an agency could voluntarily agree to adhere to them as a condition of accreditation. Becoming a foster parent requires substantial formal training and intensive background evaluations and interviews. Private agencies can also impose regulations beyond those required by the government. Agencies will often have internal grievance mechanisms to deal with foster parent complaints or adverse agency action.

States have an administrative process to challenge applicant rejection and refusal to renew or terminate foster parent status. For examples of cases addressing the rights of applicants, see *Doe v. County of Centre*, 242 F. 3d 437 (3d Cir. 2001), reversing 80 F.Supp. 2d 437 (M.D. Pa. 2000) (Agency rejection of HIV-positive applicant may violate Title II of the Americans with Disabilities Act, 42 U.S.C. §§ 12131-34 and other anti-discrimination laws). (For the denial of injunctive relief to the foster parent see 60 F.Supp. 2d 417 (1999). *Wilkerson v. State Dept. of Health and Soc. Services*, 993 P.2d 1018 (Ak. 1999) (There is no constitutional right to be foster parent; automatic denial of applicant for "serious offense" does not violate equal protection or due process given the state's interest in protecting children and the minimal economic impact on the applicant.)

D. Foster Parents' Status in Court

Foster parents are usually not parties to court proceedings regarding their foster children. (Party status means being on equal legal footing with the child, biological parents, and the government.) If they are parties, however, they may also be represented by counsel. Lack of party status does not mean that foster parents do not attend or participate in court and other formal proceedings. Even if they are not parties, they still can retain counsel and their attorney can attend proceedings, but it is unpredictable what role the judge would allow the attorney to play.

The Adoption and Safe Families Act (ASFA) (and prior to ASFA many states) provided certain procedural and participation rights to foster parents. Usually these procedural rights are limited to notice of important events and the right to be present. ASFA and many state statutes use the phrase "right to be heard." Some statues use the word "participate." The scope of the term "right to be heard" and "participate" is flexible. "Participate" can range all the way from speaking on the record or submitting reports to actually calling witnesses and attempting forcefully to affect the planning for the child. The "right to be heard" can be similarly interpreted.

In re Destiny S., 639 N.W.2d 400 (Neb. 2002) is instructive as an example of legal and factual factors which impact participation in a proceeding and the distinction between participation and a right to be present. *Destiny S.* involved a contest between a "great grandmother" to regain custody of her great granddaughter after the great granddaughter had been adopted and then relinquished for adoption by the adoptive parents. Any rights possessed by the biological great grandparent had been extinguished by the adoption. In analyzing the factors the court discussed the realities of participation by "great

grandparents" quoting from the lower courts determination that great grand-
mothers were

> parties of interest, only as it applies to their qualification to serve as
> a placement for Destiny, and therefore, may present evidence re-
> garding their qualifications. They are not parties of interest 'allowing
> discovery, questioning, cross-examining, or calling witnesses beyond
> that which is personally applicable to their qualifications for consid-
> eration by the court.'[6]

This subject is also discussed in Chapter Six, Court Process.

E. Foster Parents and Foster Children: Are They Family?

In *Smith v. Organization of Foster Families for Equality and Reform,* [O.F.F.E.R.]
431 U.S. 816 (1977), the U.S. Supreme Court addressed the constitutional rights
of foster parents to a hearing regarding removal of the child from their home.
The foster parents argued that they had what is known as a "substantive right",
in this case a right to a continued relationship with their foster children. A "right
to a relationship" backed by the Constitution would enable the foster parent to
contest the foster child's removal by forcing the agency to prove that removal
was either legally required or necessary to promote the welfare of the child. In
other words, a substantive right held by the foster parents would limit the
agency's right to sever the relationship. The Supreme Court rejected the foster
parents' position. Subsequent to *Smith* some courts have concluded that foster
parents do have a constitutionally protected interest in a relationship with the
foster child though other courts have concluded the opposite.[7]

  Rodriguez v. McLoughlin, 214 F.3d 328 (2d Cir. 2000) sheds some light on the
impact of *Smith v. O.F.F.E.R.* and on the rights of foster parents in general and
"long-term" foster parents who are adopting their foster children. Andrew the
child, had lived almost his entire life in the home of the plaintiff. As his adoption by the plaintiff was about to become final Andrew was removed from the
foster home. Subsequently, after several months, Andrew was returned and the
adoption was granted. Sylvia Rodriguez, the foster-adoptive parent argued that
the refusal to allow visits after the removal, and the delay in providing a hearing to contest the removal and obtain the return of Andrew, violated her rights.
She argued that she and Andrew should have been treated as a biological family. The defendants argued that since adoption proceedings were not final, Rodriguez and Andrew did not have any such rights.

  The Federal District court ruled in favor of the foster mother Rodriguez
and found that she had a right to protect the "stability and integrity of the re-

lationship" between herself and Andrew. On appeal the U.S. Circuit Court of Appeals reversed and found that, at the time of Andrew's removal neither he nor his foster mother had any rights regarding living together or post-removal visitation. The court reasoned that such rights could be created, if at all, under state law and not the Constitution. Reviewing New York state law, the court found that the regulatory and statutory provisions relied upon by the District Court created procedural rights or preferences but not substantive rights. That is, the court found nothing in state law that limited "official discretion with respect to matters of removal or visitation." The court placed great emphasis on the language of the Adoptive Placement Agreement, especially the clause that read

> that if at any time prior to the legal adoption 'it is determined by the agency or' by Rodriguez that the child should be removed from the foster home, Rodriguez would cooperate with the agency in carrying this out in a way that serves the best interest of the child 'in the judgment of the agency'.

Rodriguez is but one examples of a court's assessment of foster parents' rights when it comes to protecting and preserving their relationship with a foster child. It demonstrates not only the uncertainty of the law in this area but also how important the "right to a relationship" issue is to foster care agencies, foster parents, and children.

The lack of a right to a relationship does not enable the state to arbitrarily remove a child from a foster home without some process in place to allow the foster parent to challenge that removal. For example, District of Columbia law provides that if a foster child is going to be removed from a foster home in non-emergency situations the foster parents must be given notice and an opportunity to challenge the removal. D.C. Code §16-2320(g).

F. Foster Parent Obtaining Custody or Guardianship of a Foster Child

Another issue that surfaces is the authority or right of a foster parent to obtain legal custody of a foster child.[8] If current trends are any prediction of the future it can be expected that foster parents will be viewed as people who can be responsible for far more than merely providing food, clothing, shelter, and discipline. Instead, foster parents will be an integral part of the team that is charged with seeking the objectives of the case plan. As a result, the foster parent will have much greater influence over the planning for children. It will be necessary for foster parents to have far more authority and far more discretion. A possible outcome would be granting a foster parent some form of legal custody, or in some circumstances, even guardianship.

G. Foster Parents as Adopters

Some states prohibit foster parents from adopting without prior permission of the agency, but sometimes courts do not allow enforcement of such statutes or regulations. *In re McDonald's Adoption*, 274 P.2d 860 (Cal. 1954) (Adoption granted without agency consent); *In re Adoption of Alexander*, 206 So.2d 452 (Fla. App 1968) (Adoption granted despite foster parent-agency agreement that foster parents would not petition to adopt); *Oxendine v. Catawba County Dept. of Soc. Serv.*, 281 S.E.2d 370 (N.C. 1981)(Foster parent agreement not to adopt not enforced).

III. Conclusion

Laws relating to foster parenting continue to evolve through judicial opinions, new state and federal laws, and changes in the foster parent-foster agency contractual relationship. It is difficult to predict the future but the trend is for the authority of foster parents to increase thus leading to greater responsibility and greater accountability. This trend in turn will increase the liability exposure of foster parents. The response to this increased liability exposure should engender state-created or subsidized insurance programs or other mechanisms that will protect foster parents accused of negligence and provide compensation to injured children when necessary.

3

Biological Parents

CHAPTER GUIDE

I. Overview

In contrast to children with neglect-abuse cases, who have very few rights substantial enough to attract the protection of the U.S. Constitution, biological parents are favored with strong constitutional protections to raise their children free from government intervention. A long line of U.S. Supreme Court cases defines the rights of parents to make private choices about their children's education, religion, and health care—even when those choices are at odds with prevailing standards in public life. It is only when children are, or may be, seriously harmed by their parents' choices that parental rights over children can be modified by state action, and then only if the parents are accorded due process of law.

What is the process of law due a biological parent? The 14th Amendment states in pertinent part:

> All persons born or naturalized in the United States, and subject to the jurisdiction thereof, are citizens of the United States and of the state where they reside. No state shall make or enforce any law which shall abridge the privileges or immunities of citizens of the United States; nor shall any state deprive any person of life, liberty or property, without due process of law; nor deny to any person within its jurisdiction the equal protection of the laws.

In 1923, the U.S. Supreme Court decided that the word "liberty" as applied to families refers not just to physical liberty, but to an individual's freedom to act, for example, to make contracts and acquire knowledge. *Meyer v. Nebraska,* 262 U.S. 390 (1923). In 1925, the Supreme Court in *Pierce v Society of Sisters,* 268 U.S. 510, determined that parents could decide how their children would be educated, barring the state from "standardizing" the children by compelling public education. Two decades later, *Prince v. Massachusetts,* 321 U.S. 158 (1944), clarified that parental choices were not absolutely protected even when accompanied by a claim of religious freedom. If a child's welfare were endangered by her parents' religious practices, she could be protected by the same laws applicable to other parents. These three cases—*Meyer, Pierce,* and *Prince*—create the tension that pervades foster care law today. Judges in later cases have had to ask: at what point does a child's endangered welfare limit the choices that a parent may make under protection of the U.S. Constitution?

Although the Court has not been entirely consistent in the years since, the basic rights of parents to raise their children have been upheld. *Wisconsin v. Yoder,* 406 U.S. 205 (1972), prevented the state from interfering with a parent's choice regarding education when that choice is accompanied by a claim of religious freedom. Recently, *Troxel v. Granville,* 530 U.S. 57 (2000) determined that a judge could not force a parent to relinquish her children for periods of visitation with their grandparents. There has been some sliding in the other direction: notably *Lassiter v. Department of Social Services,* 452 U.S. 18 (1981), which refused to require counsel for indigent parents at termination of parental rights (TPR) hearings. In contravention to *Meyer*, the Court stated that the 14th Amendment's word "liberty" refers only to physical freedom. Parents are not jailed if they lose a TPR case, therefore indigent parents as a class are not entitled to state-subsidized legal representation, though a judge might decide that parents in a particular case should have representation. Nevertheless, the dominant theme has been to protect the private relationship of parents with their children. For example, in adoption cases unmarried fathers have the same right married fathers to a full hearing on the issue of parental fitness before termination parental rights. *Stanley v. Illinois,* 405 U.S. 645 (1972). The state's proof of parental unfitness must be "clear and convincing." *Santosky v. Kramer,* 455 U.S. 745 (1982).

While the Supreme Court cases describe broad due process rights for parents, once a neglect-abuse case enters the foster care - court system, parents' actual interaction with their children can be modified. It is often not the status of the case or the legal mandates that determine the extent to which parents can continue to be involved in their children's lives. Rather, parents' access to their children can depend on cooperation with the social worker, foster family, and judge's orders. Barriers to visitation can be raised even prior to an evidentiary hearing (for example, if the parent is dangerously aggressive toward the child), while visitation and other privileges may be allowed even when the parent's rights are about to be terminated (for example, if the parent has a positive relationship with the children even though she is unable to care for them).

Federal laws and most state laws describe the following categories of parental interaction with a foster care system:

Voluntary Placement: Parents can request help from a state's child protection or foster care agency. Usually a contract, called in federal law a voluntary placement agreement, is signed. It describes the services the agency will provide and the duties of the parents to strengthen their family's situation and visit the children. 42 U.S.C. §672(f). This agreement permits the agency to receive federal funds for the services it provides. Parents may receive a variety of aid, including child care, help to access social benefits like food stamps or special education, temporary placement of the child away from home, and so forth. The agreement expires at the end of 180 days and the child is returned to the parents, unless the agency takes the case to court, alleging that the parents are unable to adequately care for the child. 42 U.S.C. § 672(e)

Emergency Placement: A crisis may arise that requires the child protection system to quickly intervene: for example, if a young child is found on the street without adult supervision, or a parent is killed leaving the child without immediate protection. If the child is not returned home quickly, the agency that removed the child is required to initiate a court case within a time specified in state law, usually within 24, 48, or 72 hours.

Dependency Case Initiated: The parents are alleged to have neglected, abused, or abandoned the child, but the case has not proceeded to an evidence-based court finding. Once the case enters the court system, the judge or magistrate in most states has a significant role in determining the conditions applying to a parent's interaction with the child. The judge will consider recommendations from the foster care agency, counsel for the parents, the child's representatives, possibly psychologists or other experts, and perhaps other witnesses. The judge then makes a decision about whether the child will live at home or in a kinship or foster home, and what degree of contact the parents will have.

Neglect, Abuse, or Abandonment Found by the Court: When the court determines that the child is, or imminently will be, endangered in her parents' care, the foster care agency typically will try to reunify the family, possibly with concurrent efforts to find a permanent out-of-home solution, such as adoption or relative placement. The parents' cooperation with social workers and adherence to the case plan and judge's orders usually is crucial to achieving reunification as a permanency goal. Once a formal finding of neglect or abuse occurs, state law varies as to how great the judge's role is to determine conditions of interaction with the child. In some states, this determination is left entirely to the foster care agency, while in other states the judge continues to make decisions based on information received at the review hearings.

Permanent Disposition: At the 12-month permanency hearing, if reunification efforts end and the child is placed away from the parents' home, the amount of contact the parents have with the child depends on the type of placement and the wishes of the permanent caretaker. If kinship care or permanent guardianship is the outcome, parents can hope to negotiate a continued relationship. If the decision is adoption, however, a termination of parental rights hearing or an actual adoption follows. The foster care agency often continues to have legal custody of the child until the permanent placement is secured, so the parents' cooperation with social workers can influence the degree of contact.

Termination of Parental Rights: If a government's action to terminate parental rights is successful, the parents' rights to direct any aspect of the child's life ceases unless special conditions are agreed to in an "open" adoption. (Open adoption is a status permitted in some states where a degree of continued parental contact is negotiated). The child will be adopted, or another permanent living arrangement will be developed. (Court process is described more fully in Chapter Six.)

II. Significant Legal Issues

A. Visiting

Visitation between parents and children in foster care is a dominant issue in many foster care disputes. Either the foster care agency complains that the parents do not visit consistently or often enough, or the parents complain that the children are being kept from them, visitation is not frequently or conveniently scheduled, or it is oversupervised. Whether a parent's rights should be terminated can be decided just on the issue of visitation. As a Virginia parental rights termination statute states in pertinent part at 16.1-283.(c)(1):

> Proof that the parent or parents have failed without good cause to communicate on a continuing and planned basis with the child for a period of six months shall constitute prima facie evidence of this [abandonment] condition.

But is visitation an actual right belonging to parents whose children have been put in foster care? One can search U.S. Supreme Court cases without finding any direct description of a right of visitation during foster care. In The Adoption and Safe Families Act (ASFA), where reunification services are described by type, there is no mention of visitation. 42 U.S.C. §629a(a)(7). In Virginia, as in some other states, visitation is described as if it were a right (Code of VA 16.1-228), but other parts of the same code explain how visitation can be modified or entirely taken away when parents do not adhere to the case plan or fail to cooperate with social workers and court orders. It may be more accurate to consider visitation to be a responsibility, or a privilege that can be forfeited.

The terms and conditions of visitation are negotiated with the foster care worker, and usually set forth in the contract between the agency and the parents (the case plan). In states that grant the power to courts to intervene, predisposition disputes can be resolved by a judge. (As discussed in Chapter Six, II.A, state case law and statutes determine how much power the judge has over post-disposition foster care arrangements.) If the parties end up in a termination of parental rights action, visitation will be a fundamental element in the case. The court will look at both the case plan and the termination statute to see what is the required amount and quality of visitation.

A few parental termination statutes are specific. For example, Wisconsin Stat. Ann. 48.415(1)2 states what will happen if "the parent has failed to visit or communicate with the child for a period of 3 months or longer." Laws in some other states refer back to the case plan, for example, Colorado Rev. Stats. Ann. at 19-3-604(1)(c)(I)(A): "The parent has not attended visitations with the child as set forth in the treatment plan, unless good cause can be shown for failing to visit." A Virginia statute lays out the elements to be balanced at 16.1-283(c)(1):

> The parent or parents have, without good cause, failed to maintain continuing contact with and to provide a substantial plan for the future of the child for a period of six months after the child's placement in foster care, notwithstanding the reasonable and appropriate efforts of social, medical, mental health or other rehabilitative agencies to communicate with the parent or parents and to strengthen the parent child relationship.

An examination of termination of parental rights statutes can sometimes offer the best way for counsel and parties to understand the law's requirements for parental visitation.

A series of California cases show how courts accumulate the elements that go into visitation. These cases are well described by Judge Leonard Edwards, in *Judicial Oversight of Parental Visitation in Family Reunification Cases,* 54 Juvenile and Family Court Journal, No. 3, Summer 2003 at 1. In 1990 the California Court of Appeals clarified that:

> ...the determination of the right to visitation and the frequency of visitation are a part of the judicial function and must be made by the court; however implementation of the court's order may properly be delegated to an administrative agency such as the Department of Social Services.

In re Jennifer G., 270 Cal. Reptr. 326, 327 (Cal.Ct.App.1990). In 1996 the court decided that although placement with kin was an important element of a reunification plan, children could not be placed with kin so far away that frequent visitation by the parent would be impracticable. *In re Luke L.,* 52 Cal.Rptr. 2d 53 (Cal.Ct.App.1996).

In 1997 the court dealt with the complex matter of whether private therapists could be given the power through a court order to deny visitation altogether. The appeals court drew a line at giving private therapists that power. Since private therapists are not legally bound to act on behalf of the Juvenile

Court, they cannot be given unlimited discretion to make visitation decisions. "Although a court may base its determination of the appropriateness of visitation on input from therapists, it is the court's duty to make actual determinations." *In re Donnovan J.,* 68 Cal Rptr 714 (Cal.Ct.App.1997).

In 1998 the California Court of Appeals dealt with the case of a small child whose mother was incarcerated for some months in jail. The social service agency recommended that there be no visitation because the jail environment might not be good for the child. In California, infants and small children can be fast-tracked to a permanency decision in six months. The court observed that reunification would be impossible, given the tight statutory timelines, if the child and mother could not visit in jail. It therefore decreed that the government would have to demonstrate "by clear and convincing evidence that visitation with the incarcerated parent would be detrimental to the minor." *In re Dylan T.,* 76 Cal. Rptr 684 (Cal.Ct.App.1998).

In 1999, the court considered whether a child could be given absolute veto power over parental visitation. The mother in this case frightened her children by stalking them and behaving erratically while they were in foster care. Nevertheless, the court reaffirmed that "the ultimate supervision and control over this discretion must remain with the court, not social workers and therapists, and certainly not with the children." *In re Julie M.,* 81 Cal Rptr. 2d 354 (Cal.Ct.App.1999).

As in California, each state has a body of visitation cases. By analyzing the most recent cases together with state statutes and court rules, the practitioner can gauge the court's attitude toward parent—child visitation.

B. Participating in Important Decisions for Children

Parents do not lose their parental rights except through relinquishment, adoption, or a judicial order terminating those rights, an order that creates complete legal separation between the child and parents. Therefore, while the children are in foster care, parents retain something that many state statutes refer to as "residual parental rights." For example, D.C. Code §16-2301 (22) states:

> The term "residual parental rights and responsibilities" means those rights and responsibilities remaining with the parent after transfer of legal custody or guardianship of the person, including (but not limited to) the right of visitation, consent to adoption, and determination of religious affiliation and the responsibility for support.

These inchoate rights have never been defined in a U.S. Supreme Court case. They are generally understood to be those rights identified in the foundation U.S. Supreme Court cases of *Meyer, Pierce,* and *Prince:* religion, health, and education. Yet again and again when parents have tried to assert these rights to affect foster care decisions about placement, schooling, and medical care, courts have ruled that the agency's need to make "best interests" decisions for the children in their care overrides the wishes of parents who are at least alleged to be unfit, unless those parents' wishes can be met conveniently. This point of view is well expressed in *Wilder v. Bernstein,* 848 F. 2d 1338, 1346-7 (2nd Cir. 1988), which said:

> It is one thing to recognize the right of parents to choose a religious school for their children as a private alternative to meeting state-imposed educational requirements in public schools. It is quite another matter, however, to suggest that parents who are unable to fulfill their parental obligations, thereby obliging the state to act in their stead, at their request, or involuntarily, nonetheless retain a constitutional right to insist that their children receive state-sponsored parenting under the religious auspices preferred by the parents. So long as the state makes reasonable efforts to assure that the religious needs of the children are met during the interval in which the state assumes parental responsibilities, the free exercise rights of the parents and their children are adequately observed.

The *Wilder* court suggested that "reasonable efforts" could include providing funds for religious instruction. As the federal Eastern District Court of Virginia put it in *Pfoltzer v. County of Fairfax,* 775 F. Supp. 874, 885 (1991), "...a state has no duty to place a Buddhist child with a Buddhist foster family, a Quaker child with a Quaker family, or a Zoroastrian child with a Zoroastrian family, unless such a family is reasonably and immediately available." The Third Circuit agreed in *Walker v. Johnson,* 891 F. Supp. 1040, 1048 (M.D. Pa, 1995), saying:

> The overall best interests of the child must predominate. If, for example, when the child is placed in foster care, a foster family or institutional program is immediately available that would meet all of the child's needs, but is of a different faith, rarely, if ever, would the religious difference justify not placing the child in that program or with that family, thereby depriving the child of a chance to thrive in a setting otherwise ideally suited to its needs.

See also *Bruker v. City of New York,* 92 F. Supp 2d 257 (SDNY 2000).

As with issues about child care and education, many health care controversies arise in a context of religion. When parents assert religious objections to the medical care of their children in foster care (for example, Jehovah's Witnesses object to blood transfusions), courts often refer to *Prince v. Massachusetts*, 321 U.S. 158 (1944). The Supreme Court established that there are limits to a parent's authority, such as when a child is at risk for a communicable disease that can impact a whole community. See Marjoire J. Shields, *Power of Court or Other Public Agency to Order Vaccination Over Parent's Religious Objection*, 94 ALR5th 613 (2001; Supp 2003); Jay M. Zitter, *Power of Court or other Public Agency to Order Medical Treatment Over Parental Religious Objections for Child Whose Life is not Immediately Endangered*, 21 ALR5th 248 (1991).

Of course, parents have raised barriers to their child's health care without the element of religious objection. Often the potential risk the medical procedure poses to the child is weighed against the potential risk to the child if the treatment does not proceed, with a slight tendency to honor the parents' wishes if the health outcome is uncertain. E.g., *A.D.H. v. State Dep't of Human Resources*, 640 So.2d 969 (Ala.App. 1994); *Matter of Christine M.*, 595 N.Y.S. 2d 606 (1992); *In re Phillip B.*, 156 Cal. Reptr. 48 (Cal.Ct.App.1979), *cert den.* 445 U.S. 949; *In re Hudson*, 126 P. 2d 765 (Wash. 1942). See John C. Williams, *Power of Court or Other Public Agency to Order Medical Treatment for Child Over Parental Objections not Based on Religious Grounds*, 97 ALR 3d 421 (1980; Supp. 2003).

C. Agency's Reasonable Efforts to Reunify the Family

Under The Adoption Assistance and Child Welfare Act of 1980, P.L. 96-272, which preceded ASFA, the requirement that child protection and foster care agencies must make reasonable efforts to reunify a family became a main— and in some states very successful — defense to termination of parental rights actions, as well as a major delay in moving children into permanent placements. Believing that the reasonable efforts requirement had been misinterpreted, Congress described in ASFA the kinds of services the agency must provide, a front loaded procedure for service delivery, and shorter time limits for providing them. A number of exclusions were created. Under ASFA, the only parents certain to receive reunification services are those who show an early capacity to adequately function as a family, do not have a record of chronic child abuse, or violent behavior toward their other children, and whose parental rights have never been terminated. Discretion lies with the court to provide reunification services to other families, although ASFA decrees that some violent parents must forfeit services altogether. 42 U.S.C. §471(a)(15)

1. Services offered

Reasonable efforts must be made by the child protection agency to prevent removal of a child from home, or in lieu of reasonable efforts, a report on why these services could not be offered must be submitted to the court (describing, for example, why the crisis was so immediate and severe that the child had to be removed at once). Appropriate preventive services are listed in the part of the Social Security Act known as the Promoting Safe and Stable Families legislation, 42 U.S.C. §629a(a)(1)-(2). Among specific services mentioned are parenting classes and respite care. Preventive services are applicable to pre- and post- foster care status.

More significant to parents whose children are in foster care are the specific services described in ASFA to reunify qualified families (that is, families that have not been excluded from this benefit). Found at 42 U.S.C. §629a(a)(7) these include:

- Individual, group, and family counseling
- Inpatient, residential, or outpatient substance abuse treatment services
- Mental health services
- Assistance to address domestic violence
- Services designed to provide temporary child care and therapeutic services for families, including crisis nurseries
- Transportation to or from any of these services and activities

These services are phrased as if they are mandatory ("Reasonable efforts shall be made...." "Services and activities are the following....") but obviously a court would require them only if the services fit the need. Promotion of the child's safety and wellbeing is the overarching standard such services must meet.

Even if a parent qualifies for reunification services, the agency need not put all—or any—of its reasonable efforts toward that goal. ASFA encourages the agency to develop concurrent plans for an out-of-home placement in case reunification fails. And if reunification is viewed as unlikely, or if the parents stumble during the allotted time, the agency's reasonable efforts can be directed entirely toward an out-of-home placement. The effect is to put much more of the reunification burden on the parents, shifting it away from the agency.

2. Time limits

Reunification services for a family are not to be extended beyond a fifteen-month period that begins when the child first enters foster care. 42 U.S.C. § 629b. The beginning date is the earlier of (1) the date of the first judicial finding of neglect-abuse or 2) the date that is 60 days after the child's removal from home, 42 U.S.C. §675(5). State laws may tighten time frames even more. The fifteen months can be tolled during trial home visits. For example, suppose a child was in foster care for seven months, then had a trial home visit for two months, and had to return to foster care. The fifteen-month period conceivably could be extended by two months.

The general tendency of ASFA however is to tighten rather than extend time limits. A permanency plan must be developed within 12 months of the child entering foster care (subject to three exceptions: "compelling reason," kinship care, or failure of agency's reasonable efforts). If any of the exclusions come into effect, or if a court simply decides it is in the child's best interests, a termination of parental rights petition can be filed within 30 days of the child's entry into foster care. 42 U.S.C. §671 (a)(15)(E).

3. Exclusions

ASFA describes the kind of parents who can be denied reunification services. Specifically, ASFA states an agency "shall not be required to provide services," apparently leaving an agency the discretion to nevertheless offer services in certain situations. 42 U.S.C. §671 (a)(15). Parents who can be denied reunification services are those who have:

- subjected a child to aggravated circumstances, at minimum including abandonment, torture, chronic abuse, and/or sexual abuse;
- murdered or caused voluntary manslaughter or serious bodily injury to a parent's other child; or aided, abetted, conspired, or attempted such; or
- had parental rights involuntarily terminated as to another child.

The last item, as well as the reference to "chronic abuse" suggests that parents who cycle through the neglect-abuse system more than once are in danger of having their parental rights terminated soon after another of their children enters the foster care system. In fact, these exclusions are extended further by the legislative "rule of construction" that permits states to terminate parental rights early for other reasons, or because it is determined to be in the child's best interests. §103(d) of the Act.

Given all the exceptions to an agency's obligation to make reasonable efforts to reunify a family, how solid is a biological parent's claim for services to reunify the family? The answer is that families entering the foster care system for the first time have strong claims to specific services right away. Their responsibility is to prove themselves willing to put those services to good use. Basically, they have a year to prove themselves, unless (1) there are trial home visits that extend the time; (2) a court agrees with a foster care agency that there are "compelling reasons" why the time can be extended; (3) the child can be placed with relatives; (4) or the parents can prove that reasonable efforts were not made to reunify the family. 42 U.S.C. §675(5)(E). However, parents with a history of court involvement in the neglect-abuse system, or who are demonstrably violent, or even who previously resisted giving up another child and had parental rights involuntarily terminated, are at risk to lose their children quickly.

4. Extension of deadlines; elimination of mandates

a. Compelling reason

The term "compelling reason" is used in the ASFA statute to mean development of a permanent placement different from the four standard ones otherwise required. Other than stressing that the compelling reason must be well documented and in the best interests of the child, the statute does not elaborate. Here is the pertinent language.

> In the case of a child who has been in foster care under the responsibility of the state for 15 of the most recent 22 months…the state shall file a petition to terminate the parental rights of the child's parents… unless—…
>> (ii) a state agency has documented in the case plan (which shall be available for court review) a compelling reason for determining that filing such a petition would not be in the best interests of the child…. (42 U.S.C. §675(5)(E))
>
> …a permanency hearing…shall determine the permanency plan for the child that includes whether, and if applicable when, the child will be returned to the parent, placed for adoption and the state will file a petition for termination of parental rights, or referred for legal guardianship, or (in cases where the state agency has documented to the state court a compelling reason for determining that it would not be in the best interests of the child to return home, be referred for termination of parental rights, or be placed for adoption, with a fit and willing relative, or with a legal guardian) placed in another planned permanent living arrangement….42 U.S.C. §675(5)(C)

HHS offers a few examples of what a compelling reason could be in its regulations interpreting the statute at 45 C.F.R. §1356.21(h)(3), including the preamble at 65 F.R. 4058-4059 (January 25, 2000). It emphasizes that the term is to be kept flexible to cover exigencies that cannot be foreseen. The three examples are:

1. an older teen seeking emancipation;
2. existence of significant parent-child bond though the parents cannot care for the child; and
3. a tribal alternative for a Native American child.

There has been much discussion about whether permanency deadlines could be extended on the basis of a compelling reason, for example, if a mother was close to completing substance abuse treatment but needed a few more months before she could resume parenting. There is not yet enough case law to provide guidance in this area.

b. Kinship care

Although adoption is the legislatively-favored legal status for children who cannot be reunited with their parents, if a child is placed with kin, a termination of parental rights statute need not be filed. The child's placement with kin must be "at the option of the state." 42 U.S.C. §675(5)(E)(i).

c. Agency's insufficient reasonable efforts

A permanency plan for a child lists the services that an agency will offer to parents to reunify the family. If those services are not in fact delivered, or they are offered in an inaccessible way (for example, at inconvenient times or at distances beyond the parent's reach), a parent could argue that the mandatory deadlines for TPR should not be imposed. 42 U.S.C. §675(5)(E)(iii).

d. Trial home visits

Trial home visits, while not referenced in the ASFA statute, appear in the HHS regulations interpreting the statute. A trial home visit cannot exceed six months, unless a court sets a different end date. 45 C.F.R. §1356.21(c). Legitimate trial home visits are explicitly excluded from calculation of the deadline for a permanency decision. 45 C.F.R. §1356.21(i)(1)(i)(C). They extend the statutory deadline by the same length of time as the visit.

e. Runaway episodes

The same regulation that excludes trial home visits from the calculation of a permanency deadline also excludes periods when the child has run away from a foster placement. 45 C.F.R. §1356.21(i)(1)(i)(C).

D. Due Process

The major due process issues for biological parents in foster care law are 1) whether both biological parents are entitled to *notice* of dependency proceedings; 2) the evidentiary standard of proof in court *hearings;* 3) what *additional process* is due Native American parents and tribes; 4) whether indigent parents are entitled to *counsel* during termination of parental rights proceedings; 5) at what point may parents *appeal* a finding against them; and 6) whether parents have a right to *privately enforce* federal statutes, like the "reasonable efforts" provision in ASFA .

1. Notice

As a result of a series of U.S. Supreme Court cases, biological mothers and married fathers whose parental rights have not been modified in a court action are always due notice of dependency and parental rights termination proceedings.

Whether unmarried fathers are entitled to notice is a question to be answered on a case-by-case basis. It is settled that a state cannot exclude all unmarried fathers based simply on their unmarried status. *Stanley v. Illinois,* 405 U.S. 645 (1972). If the father has not "grasped the opportunity to develop a relationship with his child," however, he need not be included in the proceedings. *Lehr v. Robinson,* 463 US 248 (1983); *Quilloin v Walcott,* 434 US 246 (1978). Even if the unmarried father had "grasped the opportunity" to develop a relationship with the child, if another man is married to the mother, supporting the children, and petitioning for adoption, the biological father can be excluded in favor of the legitimate family unit. *Michael H. v. Gerald D.,* 491 US 110 (1989).

These are minimum standards dictated by federal constitutional law. State legislatures and courts are free to be more expansive, for example, to include all unmarried biological fathers in the required notice provision, as well as to determine the exact way notice shall be addressed. An article that helps make sense of these disparate cases is Janet L. Dolgin, *Just A Gene: Judicial Assumptions About Parenthood,* 40 UCLA L. Rev. 637 (1993).

2. Hearings

There are three kinds of hearings in the foster care process: (1) administrative reviews that usually occur in a place other than the courthouse, for instance at the foster care agency; (2) dependency court hearings; and (3) termination of parental rights court hearings.

Any parent entitled to notice of dependency proceedings also is entitled to participate in hearings. Summons may be issued for initial attendance and at hearings thereafter if a judge so decides. Attendance at all hearings usually is urged but absence is not punished unless a subpoena or other order was issued. Obviously, if a parent drops out of the process, the judge is likely to view that as lack of interest in parenting.

Hearings are linked to evidentiary standards. States are free to determine the standard of proof at all but termination of parental rights hearings. Typically, the initial hearings are to determine if there is *probable cause* to proceed. At the evidentiary hearing where the finding of neglect, abuse or abandonment may be made, the standard usually is *preponderance of the evidence,* though some states have higher standards of proof for the government to meet. The U.S. Supreme Court has determined that termination of parental rights require *clear and convincing evidence. Santosky v. Kramer,* 455 U.S. 746 (1982).[9]

During foster care, a number of administrative reviews are likely to be held. ASFA requires either a court or administrative review be held every six months in the early stages of a case and every year thereafter. 42 U.S.C. §675(5)(B)-(C). Administrative reviews are described in ASFA as: "…a review open to the participation of parents of the child, conducted by a panel of appropriate persons at least one of whom is not responsible for the case management of, or the delivery of services to, either the child or the parents who are the subject of the review." 42 USC 675(6) In other words, it is the right of parents who are engaged in a dependency proceeding to participate in administrative reviews, but it is not a mandate.

While a mother, and a father who is either married to the mother or at least significantly involved with his child, have a right to a hearing, a foster care worker and a judge may decide to fast track the parents to the TPR process. This decision might be made if they fall within an ASFA category of parents who have subjected a child or a sibling to "aggravated circumstances" like abandonment, torture, and assault, or it can happen even if parental rights to a sibling were involuntarily terminated. The foster care agency then is no longer required to make reasonable efforts to reunify the family and a hearing that strips the parents of their rights to raise the child can be held in as little as 30 days after the child is removed from the family. 42 U.S.C. §671 (a)(15).

3. Native Americans: notice and evidence

In any case involving a Native American child, the *tribe* is entitled to early notice so that its representatives can determine if the tribe wishes to intervene. The Indian Child Welfare Act of 1978 (ICWA),PL 95-608, 25 U.S.C. §1901 *et seq.* grants sweeping intervention powers at any stage of a foster care proceeding. (ICWA§101(c)), that can undo everything from a pre-hearing temporary placement to an adoption. The Act very broadly defines the children to whom it applies; for example, the tribe can remove the proceeding to its own courts even if a Native American unmarried father has given consent to adoption outside the tribe or has simply abandoned the child, and even where the mother is not Native American. *Mississippi Band of Choctaw Indians v. Holyfield,*490 U.S. 30 (1989). Therefore, it is important to notify the tribe as early as possible when a Native American child enters state foster care.

Note that a decision to place a Native American child in state foster care, rather than with the family or tribe, must be supported by *clear and convincing evidence* and a parental rights termination hearing requires proof *beyond a reasonable doubt.* (ICWA §102(e)-(f))

4. Legal representation

Are indigent parents entitled to free legal representation? In 1981 the U.S. Supreme Court answered that there was no absolute right to representation at the termination of parental rights stage. *Lassiter v. Dept. of Social Services,* 452 U.S. 18 (1981). The defendants argued that as a consequence of early cases holding parents had a Fourteenth Amendment liberty interest in raising their children, parents should have attorneys to defend them against loss of their children. Justice Stewart, writing for a divided court, said "liberty" had to be construed as physical liberty. If parents were not at risk for being locked up, then any right to legal representation would be based on a court weighing three elements: the parents' private interests, the government's interests, and the risk that failure to appoint counsel would lead to an erroneous decision. The Court thought that because the parents' interest usually is of greater weight than the state's interest and the risk of an erroneous decision exists, very often courts would decide that counsel should be appointed. Despite *Lassiter,* certain states provide for counsel by statute at the termination of parental rights stage[10] and a number of states provide for counsel during the entire dependency process.[11] Where it has been left to courts on a case-by-case basis, decisions have been both for and against appointment of counsel. See Patricia C. Kussmann, *Right of Indigent Parent to Appointed Counsel in Proceeding for Involuntary Termination of Parental Rights,* 92 ALR 5th 379 (2001).

5. Appeals

As part of due process, biological parents have the right to appeal decisions against them. Timing of the appeal is crucial. In civil cases, appeal usually occurs when an order is final. It is generally agreed that a disposition order placing the child in foster care after a finding of neglect-abuse is a final order. However, in dependency cases a final disposition order can be a long time coming while various interim placements are attempted. If appeal must wait until the judge issues a final order, parents and children could be unfairly separated a long time. The U.S. Supreme Court has not addressed this issue, but various state courts have. For example, in *In re Murray*, 556 N.E. 2d 1169 (Ohio 1990), the Ohio Supreme Court asserted that parental custody is a substantial right. Therefore, as soon as there has been a finding of neglect-abuse followed by even a temporary disposition order, appeal should be permitted. (Appeals are examined in greater detail in Chapter Six, II.C.)

In an appeal from termination of parental rights, must the state furnish a transcript of the hearing to a parent who cannot afford the considerable cost? The U.S. Supreme Court, in *M.L.B. v. S.L.J.*, 519 U.S. 102 (1996), said "Yes." The court relied on *Santosky*'s requirement that a termination case be decided on clear and convincing evidence and on *Lassiter*'s instruction to weigh a parent's interests against the state's when deciding whether to grant parental counsel to indigent parents in termination cases. The Court noted that parenting is a strongly protected status and the chance of a mistake is great. Weighed against the state's economic interest, a parent's right to defend against termination should win.

E. Challenging the Government's Case

ASFA presents so many mandates to regulate parental behavior that one can lose sight of the parent's basic opportunity to challenge the state's evidence of neglect or abuse. A parent is permitted—though not encouraged—to litigate every aspect of a neglect-abuse case. A parent may also present alternatives to the case plan and proposed disposition. The most effective way to do that is through competent legal counsel who understands the details of petitions, motions, discovery, deadlines, and appeals. However, denied legal counsel, a parent nevertheless has permission to raise any of these issues in court on her own. She may also object to the judge about incompetent legal counsel.

A sensitive area of the ASFA legislation is the potential for denying parents reasonable efforts to reunify the family if they have litigated termination of parental rights petition as to a child's sibling. 42 U.S.C. §671(a)(15)(IV)(iii). The effect of this provision can be to discourage parents from litigating a case out of fear of losing, thereby prejudicing the court against them in any later case. Thus, they might consent to adoption against their better judgment. Of course, litigation is not always the answer. Consent can be the better course. It is in difficult decisions such as these that skillful and sensitive legal counsel can give guidance.

F. Suing the State to Enforce Federal Statutes

When a state is required by federal law to provide certain services to families, may parents sue the state government if it fails to take those actions? The U.S. Supreme Court said "No," unless the legislation specifically states that such suits are permitted. *Suter v. Artist M.,* 503 US 347 (1992). In the *Artist M.* case, petitioners argued that state child welfare agencies were required to make "reasonable efforts" to reunite families, and that requirement implied a right for citizens to sue them if the state failed to make those reasonable efforts. The Court did not agree with petitioners, finding that the federal statute only required the state to present a plan to the federal government that contained a "reasonable efforts" section; it did not require the state to actually make reasonable efforts to reunite families. The *Artist M.* decision asserts that if Congress wanted citizens to be able to sue and enforce the law, Congress would have included language and procedures for doing that.

Artist M. represents the philosophy of a slight majority of a divided U.S. Supreme Court that federal legislation must specifically provide for citizen suits. A private right to enforcement will not be implied by courts. The result is that citizens cannot force states to implement the requirements of federal statutes unless those very statutes contain language that permits citizens to sue. In the future, other legislation applying to families in foster care situations also may be tested against this rubric. See Vicki Lens, *The Supreme Court, Federalism and Social Policy: The New Judicial Activism.* June 2001 Social Service Review, 318-336.

III. Conclusion

The legal stance of a biological parent in a civil neglect-abuse case is not unlike that of a criminal defendant. There are many U.S. Supreme Court cases that decree a state must accord parents due process of law before taking their child away. Yet the bias of the judge and the other parties is usually strongly against parents. A child has been hurt, neglected, or abandoned, and the mother and father are the most likely recipients of the participants' collective hostility. ASFA, the dominant statute, gives parents very little room for legal maneuvers. Its goal is the child's safety. Once a child is removed from home parents have—at the most!—one year to prove they can provide a safe place to the child can return. If they already have a dubious history with child welfare services, the time limits may be ratcheted down to six months or even thirty days. For most parents certain services will be offered to get them on their feet, but if the parent is not stable enough to take advantage of the services, the door quickly closes.

Despite the extension of due process through constitutional law, then, parents are only likely to be able to tell their story to the court and reunify their family if aided by skilled, conscientious attorneys who understand ASFA deadlines and are able to advocate for them at every stage of the case.

4

Public Foster Care Agencies

CHAPTER GUIDE

I. Overview

Every state has foster homes that provide care to children who cannot live in their own homes. These foster care systems are usually operated by a state or county government agency (or other government subdivision) as part of a larger agency that is responsible for social services for children and families. More often than not foster care would have a state-local structure. That is, a state level agency would create the legal and policy framework for providing foster care and child welfare services. This framework would include the laws, policies, procedures, regulations, and interpretive materials that address most if not all aspects of foster care, such as recruiting, training and certifying foster parents, maintaining and monitoring foster homes, responding to unusual incidents such as allegations of mistreatment, requirements pertaining to the care of foster children, and the rights and responsibilities of the agency, biological families, foster children and foster parents. Foster care would be provided, however, not by the state but by a city, county, or other local government agency. It is this local agency that actually establishes and monitors the foster homes and the foster children.

Foster care is generally divided into two major components— monitoring and quality control on the one hand and service delivery on the other. There is nothing that requires such a division however.

The laws, regulations, and policies that control foster care will differ in detail from state to state. Some states have a very detailed regulatory scheme that would, for example, precisely prescribe for the social worker how to document visits with foster children and specify the issues to be explored at each visit. Other states have regulations that leave substantial discretion to the local agency and social worker.[12]

A. Agency—Foster Child Legal Relationship

A foster care agency undertakes responsibility for the physical care of children that have been removed from their own homes. These agencies care for different kinds of children under different circumstances in a variety of settings. There are two main kinds of foster care: traditional and therapeutic. Therapeutic foster care embraces special needs, high maintenance and handicapped children while traditional embraces children without any identified special needs. The distinction between traditional and therapeutic calls for different levels of care, different foster home/foster parent qualifications and training and different levels of payment/reimbursement. However, it is being recognized that the traditional-therapeutic distinction may no longer be serving a useful purpose and in some jurisdictions where it once existed it is disappearing. Instead, agencies are creating a continuum of placement alternatives with the specific needs of the child being matched with a home that provides the level of care and services needed.

There are several ways an agency ends up caring for a child. First, parents may voluntarily place their child into the temporary care of the agency. This voluntary placement occurs when a family confronting a temporary crisis, such as sickness or homelessness, temporarily entrust their child to the care of the agency. These situations call for a limited transfer of parental authority to the agency. There almost always will be a document setting out the legal rights and responsibilities of the parents and agency. The agency and the parents ought to have a mutual understanding as to what may happen if the child is not returned to the parents after a prescribed period or if the parents fail to request the return of the child.

Foster care placements occur when an agency seizes a child in an emergency to prevent imminent harm, or to evaluate the child during an investigation of possible child maltreatment. In this situation, there would not be any transfer of parental authority or responsibility to the agency. The care provided by the agency would be of short duration either with the child returning home or alternatively being the subject of legal proceedings. Even though no parental authority is transferred to the agency, many states have laws that would permit the agency to examine the child and obtain information that would normally require parental consent. This authority stems not from the agency's temporary physical custody of the child, but from the state's power to investigate child maltreatment. For example, under Maryland law if a child maltreatment investigation is underway the agency can, under certain circumstances, remove a child from his or her home without parental consent or court permission and have the child "thoroughly examined." Maryland Family Law Article §5-709 (d).

A third way children enter foster care is when they are removed from their homes due to abuse, neglect or abandonment. After a court decides that the child shall not immediately return to the parent's home they placed into the care of the public child welfare agency. The foster care system creates legal relationships between and among the agency, the biological family, the removed children, and the foster parent(s).[13]

These relationships change as judicial proceedings develop. The authority of the parents is strongest and the authority of the state is most limited during the initial phases of the court process before child maltreatment has been proven. Once it is proven (or the parent admits) that maltreatment has occurred and once it is determined that the child will not be returning home, the state will assume a longer term obligation to care for the child and "legal custody" will shift to it. At that point, there is a significant change in the authority and responsibilities of the parents and the government.

In the future, the child may be returned home or may go to live with a relative. If this happens government involvement may or may not end. Sometimes a parent's rights might be terminated (or relinquished to the agency). If termination or relinquishment occurs, and until the child is adopted the government would exercise many of the parental rights normally held by the parents. For example, the government would have the right to consent to an adoption.[14]

The government will have a formal *legal* relationship with the foster child. This legal relationship results from the fact that the government has replaced the parent as the child's caretaker and has an obligation based primarily on statutes to fulfill the physical, emotional, and developmental needs of the child. The state's authority at this point is not the same as parental authority. For example, in most situations the state would not have the authority to withdraw life sustaining medical intervention; that remains a parental decision.

The agency-foster child relationship does not create any new legal rights for children except as it allows the child (through an attorney, guardian *ad litem* or advocate) to enforce those statutes, regulations, policies, and court orders that impose obligations on the agency. The child would have a right to require the government to properly care for him with regard to food, clothing, shelter, and education, as well as attend to his social, emotional, and intellectual development. Although there are jurisdictions that have enacted by statute or adopted by regulation or policy "foster child's rights," such "rights" are more often than not procedural (a right to be represented by an advocate or an attorney or the right to attend proceedings) or general statements of intent (a right to be cared for properly). California has enacted a "foster child's rights" statute. Section 16001.9 Welfare and Institutions Code. This statute provides that a foster child has a "right" '[t]o live in a safe, healthy and comfortable home where he or she is treated with respect" (a)(1) and "[t]o be free from physical, sexual, emotional or other abuse, or corporal punishment." (a)(2). Foster children's rights are discussed in Chapter One.

B. Agency-Foster Parent Legal Relationship

The degree of formality characterizing the foster parent-agency relationship varies from state to state and depends upon statutes, regulations, and the policies of the agency. Most states will have regulations that specify that certain information must be given to foster parents in writing early in the relationship. Usually, this document sets out the expectations and duties of the foster parents. As instances, the document could address the following; how placement decisions are made, how and why children may be removed, when to establish travel restrictions, the foster parents' role regarding parental visits, provisions for reunification with biological families, what to do in emergencies, approval or revocation of certification and grievance and appeal rights. There can, of course, be a formal contractual relationship between the foster parent and the agency. It would not be surprising if any written document signed by both the foster parents and the agency would be interpreted as a legal contract and might even be upheld in court as a contract. *Smith v. Organization of Foster Families for Equality & Reform (OFFER)*, 431 U.S. 816, (1977) is the only Supreme Court case that addresses foster parents and public foster care agencies.

The actual relationship between the public agency and foster parents differs from state to state. Foster parents can be, but usually are not, employees of the public foster care agency. They can be treated as employees for certain purposes and in certain situations, such as immunity from liability or access to insurance coverage. More often than not foster parents are not employees but are considered to be independent contractors.[15]

C. Agency-Biological Parent Legal Relationship

Once a foster care case is initiated in court the legal relationship between an agency and a biological parent is involuntary in that the parent's child is being cared for by the agency against the will of the parent. The relationship can be described as one between service provider and service recipient. The relationship is characterized by state and federal laws that impose requirements on the agency to develop a case plan and to provide services. The parent can demand enforcement of those laws and regulations that impose obligations on the agency. At the same time, biological parents are responsible for adhering to the case plan, for responding to requests from the social worker regarding visitation, following through on referrals for services, and participating in the services. At least in the early stages of a child welfare case the agency and biological parent have another relationship—the agency is the investigator of suspected child maltreatment and the parent is a possible perpetrator. This relationship is most often adversarial rather than cooperative and can thwart the agency's ability to provide help and the parent's ability or willingness to accept assistance.

There can be written agreements and informal arrangements between biological parents and agencies. There is almost always a service plan, case plan or some document that sets out the duties and obligations of the agency and parents, and will to one degree or another always affect the parent's relationship with the foster child. Although it would be hard to argue that a "case plan" is a formal contract, it does describe the nature of the relationship between the agency and biological parents.

D. Agency's Legal Relationship to Service Providers and Private Foster Care Agencies

To provide services, public agencies enter into numerous agreements and contracts with a variety of entities, such as those providing mentors, tutors, private schools, medical care, clothing, parenting classes, substance abuse programs, and therapy. There is nothing that requires any public agency to provide services from in-house staff employees or other public agencies. Outsourcing or contracting out for services is a common feature of all government agencies, including child welfare agencies. It would be a rare foster care agency that did without any private sector providers. The degree to which such services are "out sourced" is controversial and is the subject of an extensive literature. A good introduction is Elliott D. Sklar, You Don't Always Get What You Pay For: The Economics of Privatization (Cornell U. Press 2000); Susan Vivian Mangold, *Protection, Privatization and Profit in the Foster Care System,* 60 Ohio State Law Journal 1295 (1999).

The nature of the relationship between the agency and the provider is similar if not identical to the relationship created by any public agency that purchases private sector goods and services -vendor and contractor. The vendor is subject to monitoring and oversight in the context of a bidding and procurement system.

Agencies can also contract out foster care itself or different aspects of foster care. As discussed in Chapter Five addressing private foster care, the agency can contract out the actual creation and operation of foster homes. In theory, the agency can out-source all of its obligation to operate foster homes and care for foster children. The agency can even delegate to the private sector the duty to choose which homes will care for which children. The agency's relationship with service providers and private foster care agencies is complex and almost always attended by contracts that detail the nature of the relationship, including the precise services to be provided, compensation for the private agency, monitoring, reimbursement of costs, and all other matters related to foster care. Agencies often contract out specific aspects of foster care such as, the recruitment and training of foster homes or conducting home-studies of foster home applicants.

E. Agency's Participation in Court Proceedings

Agencies participate in court proceedings involving foster children. In some jurisdictions it is the agency itself that appears in court. In other jurisdictions it is the county or the state that is controlling the agency and it is that entity that appears in court. In some smaller counties, it is not unusual for the agency to hire an attorney to represent them and provide advice on an "as needed" basis. This subject is also addressed in Chapter Six.

II. Significant Legal issues

A. Liability

Public foster care agencies have the authority to remove children from their biological homes and provide care to them in agency-supervised foster homes.

When the agency fails to care for children properly, it can be sued. Public agencies care for so many children that it should be no surprise that they are sued with some frequency. The most common reasons for suit are violations of the rights of biological parents and foster children, and engaging in negligent behavior that results in injury to foster children. Suits are usually in state courts, though certain kinds of cases (e.g. civil rights, class actions) can be brought in federal court. Issues pertaining to liability and public foster care agencies are addressed in Appendix A.

B. Multi-jurisdictional Issues

Some agencies place all their children into foster homes in the same state in which the agency is located. Some agencies, however, utilize foster homes in states other than the state in which the agency is located. These foster homes may be public agency foster homes but are more usually operated by private foster care agencies. Whenever foster children that are the responsibility of one agency are placed into a foster home in another jurisdiction, problems and conflicts can occur. The Interstate Compact on the Placement of Children (ICPC) controls the placement of children across state lines.[16] The ICPC places obligations on the agency sending the child and provides authority to the receiving state to (1) have advance notice of the placement and (2) the right to prohibit the placement unless the "appropriate authority" in the receiving state determines that the placement "does not appear to be contrary to the best interests of the child." Compliance with the Compact usually is not difficult, but it does require assessing the documents and materials that will demonstrate the viability of the foster home. ICPC problems arise when a child is placed in violation of the Compact or when approval is delayed or arbitrarily denied. Note that Congress is considering ICPC reform legislation applicable to foster children that is intended to hold states accountable "for the orderly and timely placement of children across State lines. (Bill No. H.R. 4505 "Orderly and Timely Interstate Placement of Foster Children Act of 2004"). A very good resource regarding the ICPC is the "Compact Administrators' Manual" published by the Association of Administrators of the Interstate Compact on the Placement of Children. The AAICPC is an affiliate of the American Public Human Services Association in Washington, D.C. Also helpful is, Bernadette W. Hartfield, *The Role of the Interstate Compact on the Placement of Children in Interstate Adoption,* 68 Neb. Law Review 292 (1989).

Other problems arise because the standards and legal requirements in the state where the foster home is located may differ or even contradict the requirements, laws, and standards in the state that has legal responsibility for the child and which sent the child into the "foster home" state. For example, in some states an administrative finding that a parent was neglectful will automatically prevent that person from being a foster parent, while in others states it would not. The foster home and foster parents will be bound by the state law where they are located, but would also be expected to abide by the policies and regulations of the state agency that placed the foster child into their home in so far as those regulations and policies do not contravene any local requirements.

C. Permanency Planning Obligations Under ASFA

Pressure on the agency to comply with ASFA guidelines for moving children quickly through the foster care system is generated in several ways. The agency is obligated to produce a document called a "case plan" for every child in foster care. 42 U.S.C. §675(1). A case plan is a document that describes the services the agency will provide and the obligations of the parents. Each case plan is subject to a "case review system" by a court or administrative reviewer in time intervals of "no less frequently than once every six months." 42 U.S.C. §675(4). Another form of pressure is the federal government's review of the adequacy of the state's plan. In that plan, the state details such components as how many foster children it anticipates serving, the kinds of preventive and reunification services it will offer, and how it will spend its money. The state describes how it will set standards for foster homes and offer a "fair hearing" to beneficiaries with complaints. Importantly, it promises to adhere to statutory time lines by providing preventive and reunification reasonable efforts in a "timely manner in accordance with the permanency plan." 42 U.S.C. §671(a)(10)-(15) and §629a(a)(7). In that regard, it may provide for concurrent planning both for reunification and for an out-of-home placement if reunification proves impossible.

A powerful directive to the agency is found in the definition of "case plan" at 42 U.S.C. §675(1)(E). If the permanency plan is for adoption or another permanent home, rather than reunification, there must be:

> …documentation of the steps the agency is taking to find an adoptive family, a fit and willing relative, a legal guardian or another planned permanent living arrangement, and to finalize the adoption or legal guardianship. At a minimum, such documentation shall include child specific recruitment efforts such as the use of state, regional and national adoption exchanges, including electronic exchange systems.

There are at least two kinds of enforcement. The first is the court, which has legal tools to order compliance (unlike the administrative reviewer, who may nevertheless have some effect through recommendations). The court examines each case plan and holds the social worker and agency accountable for failures, omissions, and lapses. Court reviews in difficult cases can feel painful and personal to a social worker who must appear in court and very often explain failures that might actually be attributable to agency policy or the service provider. Very likely, the judge herself is being subject to an efficiency review, and she does not wish her record tainted by a recalcitrant agency.

The second kind of enforcement is through federal reviews. These can be simple reviews of documentation that the foster care agency has submitted, or an on-site selective examination of cases, provision of services, adherence to ASFA deadlines, court performance, and fiscal responsibility. The consequences of such reviews can be loss of federal money. There can also be bonuses for states that do exceptionally well by swiftly placing children for adoption. (Adoption incentives are addressed in § 473A of ASFA).

D. Obligation to Provide Health Services.

Health services are discussed in Chapter One, II.C.in the context of children's rights.

E. Funding Foster Care

Operating a foster care agency is a complex and expensive undertaking. It is no surprise, then, that the funding of foster care is quite complicated and requires a significant allocation of agency resources just to properly obtain, spend, and account for the associated revenue.

A state's expenditures for child welfare and foster care are funded through a combination of state and federal revenue streams. States have access to a variety of federal programs that can pay for foster care; for example, matching funds through Supplemental Security Income (SSI), block grants from a variety of federal agencies that can be allocated either as needed or according to a formula, Medicaid and adoption incentives. A practitioner in this area will want to become familiar with the terms "matching," "claiming," "eligibility," and "federal financial participation (FFP)". Sometimes federal funding is available only if the state "matches" the federal funding, sometimes dollar for dollar or sometimes at a higher or lower rate. "Claiming" refers to the ability of the state to ask for federal funding for certain expenses or categories of expenses. Being able to claim federal funding can sometimes depend on making the matching expenditures, but many times claiming depends upon providing services in accordance with statutory or regulatory requirements and meeting certain criteria and time lines. "Eligibility" is often used to refer to the status of the child. Sometimes the revenue available to pay for the care of a child will be federal if the child meets certain "eligibility criteria," such as entitlement to government benefits like Temporary Assistance for Needy families (TANF) or SSI. In other instances, eligibility will depend upon the child's legal status, such as whether the child has been surrendered for adoption or upon the foster parents' status, such as whether they have been properly licensed or certified in accordance with state and federal requirements.

A detailed explanation of the various revenue sources and exactly how they can be accessed and spent is beyond the scope of this book. One good introduction to this topic is The Child Welfare Financing Structure by Kasia O'Neill Murray which can be found at http://pewfostercare.org/research/docs/murraypaper2.pdf.

It is possible, however, to make some broad generalizations that would be applicable to all state foster care systems. Agencies almost always make foster care payments directly to foster parents. Kinship foster parents do not always get foster care payments, but the foster children would receive other benefits to which they are entitled, such as SSI.[17] The "foster care rate" varies depending on several factors, such as the number and age of the children, the needs of the children, and any limits that might be imposed by the funding source. These payments are designed to reimburse the foster parents for the day-to-day costs of caring for the foster child, including food, transportation, and increased water and electric use. Federal money may not be used to pay salaries to foster parents for ordinary parental duties but payments can be made to foster parents who must provide higher levels of supervision than would normally be the case. The agency pays for all other needs of the children, such as education, dental, and medical expenses. Indeed, in a fiscal sense, the agency is the child's parent and has all of those same expenses.

It makes good sense for foster care agencies to spend federal dollars instead of or in addition to state dollars. There is constant pressure on state agencies to access all available sources of federal money and finding as many ways as possible to make costs eligible for federal payments or matching funds. In addition, agencies will try to take advantage of incentive programs. For example, the federal government provides bonuses to states when they are able to increase the number of foster children who get adopted.

F. Privacy and Confidentiality

Public welfare agencies collect an astounding amount of information about parents, children, foster parents, and others when operating a foster care system. Foster parents are (or ought to be) thoroughly evaluated and assessed. Such assessments, usually referred to as home studies, contain information that is personal and even quite sensitive regarding family relations, medical and mental health history and issues. The agency will also accumulate a significant amount of information about foster children, including medical, mental health, and school records. Indeed, the agency will have the power to create and have access to all information relating to the biological parents, not only mental health, therapy, and school records, but also those generated through case-related services like treatment for substance abuse and psychiatric problems.

A constant issue in all foster care cases is the degree to which information can be disclosed and shared between and among the individuals and entities involved. This disclosure and sharing is affected by a complex web of federal and state laws and regulations. Ethical obligations and "best practices" standards of the various service providers are also part of the mix. Finally, court rules may contain prohibitions or protocols for sharing information.

Any discussion of privacy and confidentiality and foster care must begin by acknowledging the tension between a myriad of laws and legal principles that are designed to protect privacy and a service delivery system that requires the rapid sharing of accurate information. For instance, finding a suitable placement for a child requires knowing as much about that child as is reasonably possible and sharing at least some of that information with service providers and potential foster homes. On the other hand, the child might well have a legally cognizable right in maintaining his or her privacy, especially with regard to certain issues.

One way to narrow the search for applicable laws is to inquire what *activity* or *type of information* is involved. Are the parent's substance abuse records at issue? A teen's reproductive health records? School records? Criminal background checks? Once the focus is known, certain federal laws can be located.[18] Here are some:

Information-sharing among agencies:

Child Abuse Prevention and Treatment Act, 42 U.S.C. §5106a
Social Security Act, Title IV-E, 42 U.S.C. §671(a)(8),
45 C.F.R. §§1355.21; 1355.30; 45 C.F.R. §205

Substance abuse records from treatment centers:

42 U.S.C. §190dd-2 and §290ee-3
42 C.F.R. §§ 2.1 *et seq.* especially §2.14 (minor patients)

Criminal background checks

42 U.S.C. §671(a)(20

42 U.S.C. §5119 (a)—(c); 28 C.F.R. §20.1-.38

Homeless children

42 U.S.C. §5731

45 C.F.R. §1351.19(b)

Medical records

Health Insurance Portability and Accountability Act of 1996 (HIPAA) Public law 104-191[19]

67 Fed. Reg. 53182 (Aug. 14, 2002); 65 Fed. Reg. 82461 (Dec. 28, 2000);

45 C.F.R. Parts 160 and 164, especially 45 C.F.R. §164.512(e).

School and related developmental records

Family Educational Rights and Privacy Act, 20 U.S.C. §1232g
34 C.F.R. §§99.3; 99.36

Individuals with Disabilities Education Act, 20 U.S.C. §1412(c), 20 U.S.C. §1401(19);
34 C.F.R. §300.571

HIV-AIDS and other infectious diseases

Health Insurance Portability and Accountability Act of 1996, (HIPAA)
45 C.F.R. Parts 160 and 164. See especially 45 C.F.R. §164.512(e).

After the federal law is identified, the practitioner will search for additional state restrictions. For example, absent a judicial bypass provision, teens in some states are required to obtain the consent of, or notify parents, prior to having an abortion. Certain state constitutions have safeguards for privacy. (E.g. Cal. Const. Art. I §1). There is not much case law on limitations for sharing records, but it must be checked.[20] Do not forget court rules that may list which agencies can receive case-related information, and who may be admitted to a neglect-abuse court hearing. Finally, check professional obligations: Does a physician have an obligation to protect a patient's privacy? If so, is there a court process to overcome that? Must a mental health therapist divulge information relating to child abuse? Can information be obtained from a child's or parent's attorney relating to neglect-abuse?

Whether the practitioner wants to open or close the door on information, the right keys to the lock must be used. It should be noted that in the absence of research and advocacy, records will tend to flow into the court system and be more widely shared than is warranted under law.

III. Conclusion

Maintaining children in foster care is one of the most important tasks undertaken by the government. Agencies and social workers are under constant pressure to make sure that children being well cared for by responsible foster parents. The law does make this task any easier. Indeed, as ought to be evident the legal issues surrounding the operation of a public foster care agency are numerous and complicated. As a result agency administrators and social workers must not only become familiar with an array a state and federal laws and regulations but must also keep abreast of judicial opinions that can affect foster care.

5

PRIVATE FOSTER CARE AGENCIES

CHAPTER GUIDE

I. Overview

A. What is Private Foster Care?

Much of the care of children who enter the child welfare system is entrusted to private foster care agencies. Private foster care agencies are usually corporations run by a board of directors. They are staffed and managed by child welfare professionals who specialize in creating and maintaining foster homes for children. Some of these agencies are small, caring for only a few children. Some are quite large, caring for hundreds of children and often operating foster homes and group homes in several states. Some are traditional foster care agencies; that is, they provide foster care in a family-like setting to healthy children with few behavioral or emotional problems. Other agencies are "therapeutic" and provide care to special needs children, usually in a family-like setting. However, some therapeutic agencies utilize nontraditional settings to care for children, such as proctor or teaching foster homes. Other nontraditional settings include group homes or residential treatment facilities that are not usually thought of as foster care. There are also smaller innovative and experimental programs, which care for medically needy and fragile children who previously would have been permanently hospitalized or institutionalized. In this model, the agency purchases homes and recruits couples to live in the homes rent free while caring for a high maintenance child. One of the parents must be a stay-at-home parent. The couple must complete and continue to participate in extensive training and education relating to care for the child. Another model includes hiring foster parents and paying them a salary to care for children.

As demonstrated by the previous examples, clear distinctions between traditional and therapeutic care are now slowly disappearing. A trend is for children to be placed into foster homes that can address the children's specific needs without having to label or categorize the foster home. Foster homes will be utilized in accordance with the kinds of children that can be cared for in the home. The services provided will change as the child grows and develops. Payment and support services to the foster home will change over time. The goal is a continuum of levels of care and intensity of services that are linked to the specific needs of the child during the entire time the child is in care.

Foster care by private providers pre-dates government foster care. Historically, foster care was provided by nonprofit, often faith-based corporations, maintained or subsidized by a church or religious organization or funded by those motivated by charitable and religious purposes. Some agencies were exclusively foster care while others provided an array of services to children and adults.

There are private foster care agencies for several reasons. One is that they existed prior to the government's provision of foster care and simply continue to operate. Foster care is very expensive and as the need for foster care increases or decreases, the government is better able to respond by contracting with private providers as needed. A critical aspect of operating foster care is the recruitment, training, and retention of foster parents. Some experts believe that some types of organizations such as churches and faith-based nonprofit corporations and community groups have a better chance of recruiting foster parents.

The last few years have witnessed the emergence of for-profit foster care agencies. These agencies are usually larger than the traditional nonprofit one and enter into contracts to care for hundreds, if not thousands of children. There is no real distinction between nonprofit and for-profit agencies in terms of foster care itself—foster care always means finding people to care for children. If there is to be a distinction it is whether or not the profit-driven business model is so different from a nonprofit model as to affect the quality of the care received by the child. The quality of care may turn not so much on the profit-driven nature of the care but on the effectiveness of program oversight and the standards, if any, imposed on the for-profit enterprise. In any event, it remains to be seen whether or not foster care can be profitable enough to attract significant amounts of investment capital. See, Susan Vivian Mangold, *Protection, Privatization and Profit in the Foster Care System,* 60 Ohio state Law Journal 1295 (1999).

B. The Legal Relationship between Public and Private Foster Care Agencies

At some point after a child enters the child welfare system, the care of that child is transferred to the state government by law. Terms like "ward of the court" or "ward of the state" convey the fact that parental care has been replaced by the state. Consequently, it is now the government that must house, feed, clothe, educate and, in a very real sense, raise the child until such time as the child leaves the foster care system. The government, through state and local agencies, can create foster homes and services to care for such children. The government can also enter into contracts with private agencies to do the same thing. There are numerous funding mechanisms and arrangements governments use when private providers are used to provide foster care.

To begin, one needs to understand the distinction between "contracting out" foster care services and "privatizing" foster care. In contracting out, which is the most commonly used model, the public agency enters into contracts with the private agency. This contract can specify the responsibilities of the private agency. The contract would include the type of foster care, the duties of the worker and the services to be provided to the child. Such contracts can be quite detailed, specifying the exact services to be provided as well as the nature and focus of the foster care itself. For example, one typical contract defines "child care management" as a:

> ...process through which [t]he Contractor's [private foster care agency's] social worker assures that a child who is placed out of home receives the services appropriate to facilitating permanency for the child. These services include foster care placements, coordination of medical services, family visits, educational placements, psychological and psychiatric treatment, day care services, homemaker/respite

services, structured summer activities and the adherence to the Interstate Compact on the Placement of Children. Other services provided can include treatment planning, support and consultation to therapeutic foster parents, contact with the child on a weekly basis, support and consultation to the families of the child, community liaison and advocacy and being on call for crises. [21]

Different contracting models will result in different divisions of labor and responsibility. On one end of the continuum of private foster care services, the private agency simply provides a "bed" in the foster home, with the government agency providing the social work services and planning, monitoring the home, and arranging for all services. At the other end, the private agency provides the home, arranging and providing social work and other services, attending court and administrative reviews, and filing reports to the court. The government's responsibility will be to review and approve the private provider's services.

The government, however, subject to the residual parental rights retained by the parent discussed in Chapter Three, II. B. still has legal responsibility for the child. Having this legal responsibility means that the government must ensure the adequacy of the care provided. The government also retains the authority to make the recommendation to the court as to the child's permanency planning: whether to return home, be placed for adoption, remain in foster care, or remain in that particular foster home.

In a situation in which the greatest degree of discretion is given, the private agency will assign and supervise the social workers and other caregivers such as family support staff, homemakers, and mentors. The private social worker will assess the case and determine the case plan, in compliance with the Adoption and Safe Families Act (ASFA). In a variation of this model, the agency may have "family responsibility," that is provide services to other family members including parents and siblings. In this model, the agency prepares the reports, appears in court and administrative reviews, and generally advocates for the goal of its case plan. One of the most difficult aspects of foster care for the public agency is the fact that private agencies can refuse to accept children for placement or, after children are in a private agency foster home, they get expelled for a whole host of reasons. This private agency behavior places great stress, financial and administrative, on the public agency. Therefore, many public agencies are now imposing "no reject/no eject" requirements on private providers. This policy requires that a provider must accept all children within a very broad range of characteristics and cannot eject a child from their program except under the most extreme circumstances. This burden on the private agency makes it more like the public agency in terms of its responsibility to the child. "No eject/no reject" providers can be successful only by devising programs that can deliver a broad array of services that can be accessed very quickly. This model is accomplished by expanding available services and by creating subcontracts and joint ventures with other providers, both public and private.

There is no bright line that marks the limits of the authority or responsibility of the public agency or the private agency. This creates a tension between private and public child welfare service providers that is deeply and unavoidably embedded in the private-public relationship. This tension results from the fact that the public agency, which is legally responsible for the child, does not always agree with the private agency plan or services delivery. When this disagreement occurs, there is usually a procedure to address and resolve it. More often than not it is resolved informally, through negotiation or by the public agency simply imposing its position on the private agency. At times, the resolution may be imposed by court order, an informal administrative process, or a formal hearing. The private agency is expected to adhere to whatever regulations exist regarding foster care and will have to submit to oversight of its social work and plans. Private agencies jealously guard their prerogatives to determine the social work planning and maintenance of the foster home environment. Usually, it is the private agency that monitors the foster parents, the foster home, and the child. Most significantly, the private agency determines whether the foster home meets required standards, and in most circumstances whether it is the best one for a particular child. Under some regulatory schemes, it is the private agency that licenses or approves the foster home and then makes the home available to the public agency. Under this paradigm, the private agency controls the use of the home by the public agency.

Under the contracting out model, the public agency maintains legal custody of the child. A term commonly used is "commitment", that is, the child is committed to the care of the state. The public-private relationship is created and maintained by the contract and it is the implementation of the contract that allocates the decisional authority for the care of the child. The contract can call for a delegation of authority and responsibility to the private provider. Although such delegation is not complete in that the public agency (or the court) retains the power to reject the agency's case plan and goals, the public agency nonetheless will not attempt to micromanage the case.

Contracting out and privatization may appear to be the same because they share many attributes. The essential and critical distinction between the two lies in the legal relationship between child and the agency providing the care. In the contracting out model, the child has no formal legal relationship with the private agency (except that the agency has a legal duty to the child to provide adequate care in accordance with applicable law and standards). The child is in the legal custody of the public agency. It is this legal tie between the child and the public agency—and the authority and responsibility that go with it - that prevents the contracting out model from being privatization. Under the contracting out model, to put it one way, the public agency is renting a bed and buying the professional services of the private agency. The authority to make decisions for the child and the responsibilities for the outcomes rests with the public agency.

Under privatization, the legal relationship is between the private agency and the child: the private agency has custody of the child. The private agency has the legal authority to plan and make decisions for the child, and is solely accountable for those activities. To create privatization, a statute is needed to enable the private agency to obtain legal custody of the child. Then, the public agency becomes a funding source and perhaps a monitor of services. The public agency could exercise fiscal accountability through audits and review of the care provided. But, and this point is critical, there would be no decisional involvement by the public agency. The private agency would exercise its discretion to implement the case plan.

There are models that purport to be privatization that do not involve a transfer of legal custody to the private agency. However, when closely examined many alleged privatization schemes are in reality large scale contracting out. This large scale contracting out usually embraces almost all of the services and activities normally performed by the public agency once a child is removed from the biological home, including recruiting and maintaining foster homes, providing services, and achieving permanency. There are also times when the legal custody of children is transferred (or can be transferred) from the public agency to private agencies or even directly from biological parents to a private agency. For example, when a child is relinquished to a private agency, that agency has legal custody (including the right to place the child for adoption and consent to the adoption).

In any event, large-scale "real" privatization of child welfare would entail a radical shift in power and authority from the state to the private sector. The state and the courts determine when children are removed from the biological home. Once removed, the care and welfare of the child would be the responsibility of the private sector subject to judicial (and perhaps administrative) oversight. There are many who think that this degree of privatization is unwise and an abdication of the government's responsibility to children and families. Therefore, true privatization is rare, if it really exists at all. For true privatization to occur legislative action would be needed. Florida's privatization undertaking is one the most comprehensive privatizations of child welfare. The legislation creating this effort is found at Fla. Stat. Ann. §409.1671 (2003). For critical legal commentary on this legislation see, Christina A. Zawisza, *Child Welfare Managed Care in Florida: Will it be Innovation or Abdication?*, 25 Nova Law Review 619 (2001).

C. Funding Strategies

Funding mechanisms for private foster care are also very diverse. (An in-depth discussion of funding mechanisms is beyond the scope of this book.) One major model is a negotiated "daily rate" per child to care for children in foster care. The rate would vary depending on the needs of the child, with additional payments for additional services not automatically included in the agreed rate. Under this approach, the private agency invoices the public agency for the number of children cared for multiplied by the number of days of care. Included within the daily rate is a defined bundle of services, such as transportation to medical treatment, attendance at school conferences, preparation of court reports, and attendance at court. If a child receives other services not included in the bundle, they may be purchased by the private agency and billed to the public agency. In that scenario, the private agency can maintain almost total control over the cost of the services since the cost is defined by contract in advance and the public agency funds each child separately. Under this model, the private agency only gets paid when and if it cares for children.

At the other end of the spectrum is a model that involves the payment of a set amount of money to care for a maximum number of children for an agreed upon length of time. For example, the agency would be paid a lump sum amount payable in installments to care for a number of children until they exit the foster care system either by way of adoption, a return home, or aging out of the system. This payment method enables the public agency to control its costs and places the fiscal risk on the private agency. For instance, if the amount of money assumes an average stay in foster care of two years and the private agency reduces this to twenty months, then the private agency's "profit" is the four month's payment without delivering services. Obviously, in this model, the private agency has a strong incentive to control costs and move children out of foster care as speedily as possible.

Most funding mechanisms lie somewhere in between these two examples with the private agency providing many services at a fixed rate and the public agency providing unusual or extraordinary services such as intensive psychiatric care. Many public agencies are experimenting with changes in provision of funding to private agencies. Public agencies are creating incentives and disincentives designed to rationalize spending, enhance the effectiveness of the agency, and improve outcomes for children. Specific examples include awarding incentives when the private agency can increase access to federal funding streams in place of or in addition to local revenue, reducing the caseloads (and hence payments) to those agencies that fail to move children to permanency, and increasing the caseloads of those agencies that outperform other agencies in terms of better results for the children in care.

D. State Regulation of Foster Care

States have different regulatory schemes that affect how private foster care agencies are structured, operate, and relate to the public agencies and the court system. Although there are many variations, there are some common features that exist in virtually every system. Usually, states define by law what is a foster care agency (sometimes referred to as child placing agencies). An agency (or entity) cannot care for children out of the child's home without a license or permit to operate a foster care agency. These statutory and regulatory requirements and the nomenclature, and process used to obtain authority to operate a private placing agency differ from state to state. Usually, at a minimum, the requirements embrace several legal, management, child welfare, and procedural elements. For example, some jurisdictions would require a corporate structure, some restrict child placing to nonprofit agencies, some prescribe board membership and management requirements in terms of staffing. Regarding management, the requirements would address staff qualifications and duties, role and duties of the executive director and subordinates, education, and background information. The most extensive requirements usually pertain to foster care and child welfare practices. Jurisdictions vary as to the extent to which practices are prescribed and the degree to which adherence to standards created by national child welfare organizations, such as the Child Welfare League of America, is required. Regulations can for example embrace detailed requirements addressing the rights and responsibilities of foster parents, record keeping and the number and duration of visits and contacts with the children and foster family. The statutes can also provide foster parents with a grievance or appeal process to question or challenge agency actions. (See Chapter Two for a discussion for foster parents' rights).

E. Regulation of Foster Parent Training and Recruitment

An essential task of a foster care agency is its ability to recruit, train, and retain foster parents. There are entities that will perform recruitment, training, and approval, then refer the foster home to a child placing agency. These entities are not really foster care agencies since they cannot actually place and monitor children in a foster home. Foster care agencies usually view foster parents as "theirs" and will not permit any other agency to place children into that home and will not permit the foster parent to engage in any other child care activities, such as day care or the care of adults. The agency's claim on foster parents stems from the fact that the private agency expends its own resources and funds to create the available foster care placement resource and, therefore, closely guards its use.

This proprietary interest is protected in two ways. First, and most significantly, it is the private agency that in one way or another initially approves or certifies the foster home. Even though the requirements to be a foster parent are created by the state and even though it might be the state that actually grants the foster care permit, it is the private agency that controls the status of the foster parent. For example, the private agency can impose additional requirements or higher qualifications on foster parents than are required by statute or regulation. This discretion exists because the private agency has the power to determine who will be permitted to be one of "its" foster parents.[22]

Second, children cannot be placed into the foster home developed by the private agency without the agency's permission. Similarly, the foster parents cannot accept a child from any other agency. Thus, neither a foster home nor a private agency can be used arbitrarily by a public agency or the court system. The possible exception would be a contractual agreement that required the agency to accept and place children into any available suitable foster home. In this case, agency rejection would be a breach of contract. On the other hand, it is difficult to envision any circumstances in which a foster parent could be required to accept a foster child. If the agency were to attempt to force a foster parent to accept a child, the foster parents could simply voluntarily forfeit their license to be foster parents.

Although it would be illegal for private foster care agencies to discriminate, they cannot be forced to accept someone as a foster parent who does not fulfill the requirements. (In most states, any rejection is subject to administrative or judicial review.) There are very few reported cases that address a right to be or to continue to be foster parents. One such case is *Doe v. County of Centre*, 242 F.3d 437 (3rd Cir. 2001) (Agency rejection of HIV-positive foster parent may violate Title II of Americans with Disabilities Act, 42 U.S.C. §§12131-34 and other anti-discrimination laws), reversing 80 F.Supp.2d 437 (M.D. Pa. 2000), earlier proceeding 60 F. Supp 2d 417 (M.D. Pa. 1999)

F. Legal Relationship of Foster Parents to Private Agency

The legal relationship between the agency and the foster parent is similar whether the agency is a private agency or a public agency. The foster parent-agency relationship rests on some agreement between the two. The degree of formality and the detail of the agreement vary significantly. Often this agreement will spell out the relative responsibilities of the agency and foster parents. There can also be a formal contract between the agency and foster parent, especially if the foster parent is being paid to care for children as opposed to receiving funds to reimburse them for the costs of caring for the child.

Once a child is in the home, the foster parents and the agency should be in a partnership that properly cares for the child. Once again, the variations are numerous but involve the private agency assisting in referrals to services and dealing with problems. The agency also provides oversight and monitoring of the quality of care and progress toward the case plan's goal. The degree of discretion the agency accords to the foster parent varies from agency to agency and might well depend on the particular case. In other words, such decisions as choice of school or therapist may rest with the agency, but other decisions like summer camp or day care might be made by the foster parent.

The legal relationship is one of some importance, especially if the agency or foster parent is sued by the foster child or if the foster parent is injured by the foster child. The foster parent-private agency relationship is unique and is not easy to characterize in legal terms. It is difficult to fit the relationship into an existing category because it is the foster parent that actually cares for the child and who "acts as a parent," while it is the agency that is responsible for their actions and thus must exercise some control over decisions that would normally be totally within parental discretion. A fundamental question, relevant to both private and public agencies, would be whether the foster parent is an independent contractor, or an employee or agent of the agency.

The question of what is the exact nature of the legal relationship arises most often in the context of liability suits against foster parents and the agency. The issue most frequently in dispute is whether the foster parent is an employee of the agency. Indeed, this issue can determine whether the agency is liable for injuries caused by the foster parents, whether the foster parents are partially or wholly immune from suit, whether the foster parents can claim insurance coverage otherwise available to an "agency employee," and other important matters. The issue is not well settled. There are states that have statutorily defined the nature of the relationship and the rights and benefits of foster parent status in the context of a suit for damages to a foster child. The judicial opinions that have addressed this issue have reached very different conclusions.[23]

G. Oversight of Private Agency

A critical aspect of private foster care agency operations is oversight and monitoring. Private foster care agencies are affected by laws and regulations that pertain to the operation of social services agencies. Private foster care agencies that provide social services to children must be knowledgeable about state laws that affect their work. In addition, agencies must assure that their polices and procedures are in compliance with the federal laws and regulations that pertain to children, especially those that most commonly affect them on a daily basis.[24] Usually the private agencies' compliance with federal laws and mandates is achieved through internal assessments and monitoring from the public agency or licensing authority. There are several ways private agencies are monitored and regulated.

First, in most (if not all) jurisdictions private foster care agencies must be specifically approved to operate, that is, to care for children outside the children's own homes. Foster care agencies are also known as "child-placing agencies" and in many states "child-placing agencies" can provide both foster care and adoption services, that is, they can "place" children into foster homes or find adoptive homes for them. This licensing or certification system usually entails criteria and requirements for initial licensure. The specificity and rigorousness of the requirements vary greatly from state to state. Usually, the requirements embrace staffing and operational matters. Staffing would include qualifications and type of staff, adequacy of staff in terms of staff-child ratio, use and qualifications of independent contractors and part-time staff, qualifications, educational levels, experience, and supervisors. Operationally, requirements can include the development and use of policies and procedures manuals, adherence to nationally recognized standards, or the development of best practices standards. There are usually professional licensing standards for staff, requirements addressing the qualifications of supervisors, and possibly requirements tying certain tasks and responsibilities to specific qualifications.

Second, licenses must be renewed periodically. It is this renewal process that can assure a continuous monitoring of operations.

Third, in addition to or in conjunction with a renewal process, many jurisdictions provide for periodic reviews of agency operations. The intensity and consequences of such periodic reviews vary greatly. Some inspections can entail detailed review of all agency operations as well as a sample (or total) review of cases. This case review in turn can include only certain aspects of the case, such as number of visits, or the entire case. Sometimes reviews only embrace complaints or management and staffing patterns and caseload numbers. These reviews can be important to the ability of the state (or county) to assure high quality foster care. Indeed, many regulatory systems impose fines or other sanctions for failure to adhere to standards or for failure to correct past deficiencies.

Fourth, professional employees must adhere to relevant professional licensing standards. These include social workers but can also include counselors, addictions counselors, mentors, tutors, and all other staff whose ability to provide services is professionally regulated or for whom a license or certification is required.

Fifth, in addition to regulations and statutory criteria unique to foster care agencies, private agencies may also be subject to other regulations that apply to businesses or corporations in general. For example, if a foster care agency is also a corporation, it would have to adhere to the statutory requirements for corporate status. Many private foster care agencies are tax-exempt nonprofits, sometimes known as "501 (c)(3)'s." If designated a nonprofit, an agency must adhere to requirements applicable to its tax-exempt status. Such requirements pertain most importantly to fiscal matters and revenue-producing activities, as well as distribution and use of revenue.

Sixth, there are other types of regulations depending on the activities of the agency and state laws. For example, if an agency operates any group homes or shelters, those might have to obtain licenses or certificates of occupancy.

1. Who monitors the private agency?

The entity or agency that provides the monitoring also can vary. In some states, the foster care agencies are licensed and monitored by the state agency responsible for children in general or foster care in particular. In other states, this monitoring function is undertaken by a separate agency charged with all manner of regulatory affairs or by a licensing bureau agency responsible for enforcing regulations pertaining to all nonpublic entities that require state permission to operate corporate and business entities, including nonprofit or unincorporated associations.

2. Consequences of failure to adhere to standards

Failure to adhere to standards has consequences, sometimes quite dire. Sanctions can include revocation or suspension of authority to operate, refusal to renew, fines, restrictions on operations or intake (number or type of cases/children) until deficiencies are corrected, hiring consultants to assist in correcting deficiencies, increasing training, changing policies/practices, retraining staff/foster parents, more rigorous oversight, and other remedial measures.

H. For-profit Foster Care Agencies

Historically, private foster care agencies have been nonprofit operations. There is some concern that for-profit agencies ought to be monitored more strictly or even differently than the traditional not-for-profit agency. There are even some who think that for-profits should not be permitted to operate foster care agencies that care for children in the state child welfare system. It may be that for-profits have not been operating long enough for those concerned to analyze their performance. However, assuming that the standards for for-profits and nonprofits are the same, there is no apparent reason why for-profits cannot care for children in foster care just as well as nonprofits. The unease, if there is any, lies in that fact that for-profits are investor-driven designed to maximize profits, while nonprofits are (supposedly) service or mission driven. Nonprofits of course cannot survive unless revenue exceeds expenses, known as surplus. While no agency can operate for very long if its expenses exceed revenue, it is generally thought that the pressure to maximize revenue is greater in a for-profit than in a nonprofit. The biggest distinction is that the profit in a for-profit agency benefits the owners/investors whereas the surplus in a nonprofit must be used to advance the "charitable" (that is nonprofit) purposes of the agency. The debate over the use of for-profits is a continuing one with attention being focused primarily on two critical factors: Do for-profits necessarily increase the risk of poor service delivery and misuse of funds because they are (supposedly) driven more by "return on revenue" than by quality? Is the oversight by the contracting child welfare agency sufficient to ensure quality services and to detect abuse or is additional public oversight necessary? For additional insight into this subject see, Mangold, *Protection, Privatization, and Profit in the Foster Care System,*60 Ohio State Law Journal 1295 (1999).

I. New Approaches: Neighborhood Collaboratives

One of the newest developments in child welfare (and foster care) is the arrival (or as some would claim the reappearance) of the "neighborhood-based services model" and the use of what are sometimes referred to as collaboratives. A collaborative is an organization that brings together neighborhood organizations of all types to address the needs of the children and families in a neighborhood. Most collaboratives focus on children and families, while others focus on housing or economic development. In any event, a collaborative would assess the strengths, weaknesses, and resources of a community, and then marshal and allocate the resources to make the most effective use of them. The energizing force behind a collaborative is two-fold: first, to reduce the influence of the government and to empower neighborhoods and residents to take responsibility for themselves and their neighbors, and two, to reduce the number of children that are removed and placed into foster care (and when children do have to be removed to find foster homes in the child's own neighborhood). Indeed, for some collaboratives a critical measure of success is a drop in removals and an increase in children placed into the homes of relatives and friends, and whenever possible in a home in the neighborhood where the child was residing before entering the children welfare system.

Collaboratives usually turn to established traditional private foster care agencies for assistance and guidance. This collaborative-agency relationship presents challenges and opportunities. One of the most critical challenges is the need to recruit and train competent and effective foster parents in the same communities from which children are being removed from their homes. Such neighborhoods usually do not have large numbers of potential traditional foster homes. Thus, one important issue that faces a private agency assisting a collaborative in developing foster homes is the degree to which the agency can or is willing to change its criteria to approve foster homes or whether the criteria can be different for a kinship foster home. Can such changes apply to the physical size of the home, such as square feet, number of rooms, quality of neighborhood, as well as the parents themselves in terms of education, income and criminal history?

Another fruitful area of cooperation and partnership with traditional foster care agencies is the use of paraprofessionals and even lay people to assist the traditional agency in its work. Although subject to criticism by some, the collaboratives make liberal use of such people to carry out some tasks formerly only performed by licensed social workers such as supervising visits between foster children and family, transporting children, making home visits, assisting in referrals, and assessing risk situations. The traditional agency can supply the required mentoring, training, and close supervision. Sometimes, collaboratives and foster care agencies share resources and employees, and even engage in joint contracting with the county or state to supply services.

II. Significant Legal Issue: Private Agencies Appearing in Court

The degree to which private foster care agencies participate in the judicial and administrative proceedings regarding children differs from state to state. Participation is dependent upon state laws and regulations, and on the practices and policies of the states agencies and courts. The private agency social worker usually submits a written report to the court and then appears at court hearings. Sometimes the public agency will review (and may have the authority to request changes in) the written report beforehand and sometimes it will send a social worker to court as well. The situation becomes more difficult if the private agency disputes the goal with the public agency or if the public agency, either by design or chance, is not actively participating.

Practices and policies differ widely depending upon the jurisdiction, the contract or agreement between private and public agency, and the nature of the case. At one extreme is the private agency that provides services, but the public agency's social worker represents the case in court and develops and monitors the implementation of a case plan. Some systems allow, if not require, the private agency to appear in court but do not require the presence of any public agency worker or official. In some jurisdictions two workers appear, one from each agency. In some systems it is the private agency that is directly accountable to the court while in other systems the court exercises whatever control it has over the case through the public agency.

There are two aspects to the role of the private agency's provision of foster care to a ward of the state that can cause confusion. Is a private provider permitted to take a formal position regarding the nature of services to be provided or the outcome of a case? Agencies as agencies seldom have positions in a case. Rather the agency employee, the social worker, or case manager has developed a professional opinion as to the needs of the child. This professional opinion is embodied in the objectives of the case plan, as well as the methodology and services to be provided to achieve the goal. The private agency would support such a position and its social workers' opinions would be informed and shaped by the public agency's policies and practices. The social worker, however, is in effect acting as an expert advisor to the public agency and to the court. The private agency itself is not advocating a particular outcome, but providing the platform for this advice to be implemented and communicated to the court and public agency. The public agency should not attempt to influence the professional judgment of the social worker. For example, in a case in which the worker is concluding that reunification is not possible, the public agency can disagree and impose its own contrary goal but should not attempt to change the opinion of the private agency's social worker.

There are certainly situations in which the private agency's own practices and policies are at issue so that it is the agency's interests that are at stake. For example, if the private agency's own foster parents agree that they will not petition to adopt a child in their care and then later petition to adopt, this action implicates the agency's ability to enforce its relationship with foster parents. Similarly, private agencies might impose restrictions on a foster parents' practices with regard to exposing the foster child to the foster family's religious practices. A foster parents' challenge to this restriction in the context of a particular case would call into question the agency's interests.

Is a private agency a party to a foster care proceeding? (Party status means that a person has access to the full range of legal process because their interests are vitally affected by the court proceedings. Party status carries with it rights and responsibilities created by law and court practices and rules.) If the private agency is not a party by statute it can become a party to the proceeding by applying for and obtaining party status from the judge. A private agency would not need to be a party unless there were specific issue it wished to litigate. In some states it is the private agency that is allowed to initiate and prosecute proceedings to terminate parental rights while in other states they cannot. *In re Welfare of Kevin L.*, 726 P.2d 479 (Wash. Ap. 1986) (Petition to terminate parental rights cannot be delegated to a private provider); *In re Dependency of Ramquist*, 765 P.2d 30 (Wash. Ap. 1988) (Private agency had standing to file a termination of parental rights).

III. Conclusion

Private foster care agencies have been and will continue to be a critical part of the child welfare system. Indeed, it can be expected that the provision of foster care by private sector will expand in the future. This expansion will expose the private sector to increased scrutiny by the courts and public agencies and, will undoubtedly focus more attention on the legal issues relevant to private agencies.

6

COURT PROCESS

CHAPTER GUIDE

I. Overview

Child abuse-neglect courts grew from the bottom up rather than from the top down, meaning that they were not designed to fit into the logic of the existing civil system, but rather crafted to meet a pressing social need. Complexities and confusions have resulted. Viewed nationally, court processes for child abuse and neglect are a jumble of contradictory systems. Each state has its own way of processing cases, and often its own names for its procedures. Depending on how a state's legislature has set up its court system, child abuse and neglect cases might be heard in family court, juvenile court, or even in probate court. The court might be included as a division of the main trial court (eg. Nevada), or be a subdivision of a civil or family court (e.g. New York), or be located in a separate geographical place as part of a justice system that is just dedicated to children (e.g. Missouri). Certain states split the functions of child protection and termination of parental rights between two different courts (e.g. Massachusetts), or provide that the case can be heard first off the record in a lower court and, if not resolved there, formally and on the record in another court. (e.g. Virginia). In some states unified family court processes permit neglect and abuse issues to be heard in whatever forum they first arise: for example, if a juvenile delinquency case turns out to have elements of neglect or abuse, the delinquency judge may hear issues from both systems, draw on resources from both, and determine which shall be dominant. (E.g. Hawaii, Rhode Island, South Carolina, Delaware, Vermont, New Jersey) In other states there is a wall between neglect-abuse and other kinds of cases in which the same child may be involved. That wall may only be breached as court rules permit.

Because federal laws have such a powerful effect on the shape of neglect-abuse practice, cases in every state tend to flow through the court system in the same way.[24] However, state courts' names for parts of the process, and rules pertaining to interim steps like mediation and motions, can make procedures appear dissimilar from state to state. The federal government has been able to establish standards for cases because considerable financial aid is available to states that adopt the federal laws. (Examples of standards that set minimum requirements for processing neglect-abuse cases are that no federal subsidies for foster care are available under The Adoption and Safe Families Act (ASFA) unless a state has a system for reviewing the sufficiency of family case plans; and no grants are available under The Child Abuse Prevention and Treatment Act (CAPTA) unless a state's plan requires children to be represented by a guardian *ad litem,* lawyer, or court appointed special advocate.) All states have taken advantage of the benefits of federal laws. Nevertheless, as a case winds its way through state appeals, there are different interpretations of the mandated laws and there can be different outcomes as a result. For example, California has established a tight deadline of six months for family reunification with children less than three years old. Cal. Welf.&Inst.Code §361.5 and 366.21. This law is based on the ASFA rule of construction that state agencies and courts are not precluded from initiating termination of parental rights for reasons other than, or within timelines earlier than, those specified in the Act. §103 of the Act. One result could be that fewer infants return to their biological families in California than in states that permit reunification efforts to proceed over a year.

A. Roles of Lawyers, Social Workers, and Judges

Three kinds of professionals participate in nearly every foster care case: lawyers, social workers, and judges. Each represents a specific interest in the case. Each is bound by a code of professional conduct.

Lawyers serve a specific client. It is the client who determines what is to be accomplished, and the lawyer who, in consultation with the client, determines the legal means to achieve the desired outcome. American Bar Association Model Rules of Professional Conduct, Rule 1.2. Lawyers may be found in any of four roles in a case, though not all cases include lawyers in all four roles.

The government attorney (usually an employee of the state or the county) represents the government agency that is involved in a child neglect-abuse case at any particular point. When a child is in foster care, the government attorney represents the public foster care agency. The person who appears in court often is a public foster care social worker, but she may be a social worker from a private agency under contract to the public agency.[25] A government attorney does not directly represent the child. He represents the government agency that is managing the child's care.

Indigent parents are assigned counsel, paid for by the government, for critical aspects of the case. These subsidized counsel are provided under a variety of arrangements: counsel may come from a public defender service or be drawn from the private bar. They may offer partially subsidized representation to parents who have some, but not much, income. Parents with adequate income must pay for private counsel. Usually a parent wishes to keep the family unit together and continue raising her child. Sometimes, however, a parent wishes to give up her parental role. She may have a specific alternative placement in mind. Often a parent is worried about the care her child is receiving in foster care, and wishes to obtain better conditions. Parents' counsel are bound by professional ethics to attempt to achieve any legal outcome the parent requests.

A child's lawyer (as opposed to a non-lawyer advocate) may serve in either of two capacities. A lawyer guardian *ad litem* represents the child's best interests, as distinct from his legal interests. A lawyer guardian *ad litem* carries out investigations requested by the court and reports to the court. Thus, a lawyer guardian *ad litem* does not have a confidential relationship with the child.

The child may have a lawyer who represents only the child's legal interests. The lawyer maintains a confidential relationship with the child, much as she would with an adult, taking into consideration the child's age and stage of development. American Bar Association Model Rules of Professional Conduct, Rule 1.14. American Bar Association's Standards of Practice for Lawyers who Represent Children in Abuse and Neglect Cases. www.abanet.org. Obviously, older children are able to form opinions about what they want, and their attorneys are obligated to advocate for that, if it is legal. See 64 Fordham Law Review (March, 1996) for a comprehensive analysis of ethics for childrens' lawyers.

Unlike a lawyer, a social worker may represent the interests of an entire family unit when reunification is the child's ASFA permanency goal. In a foster care case "best interests of the child" is the standard to be met, so services to other members of the family would have to adhere to that goal. For example, a social worker might arrange drug treatment for a mother in the hope that family reunification could be achieved, but if the mother's treatment requires several years, with an eye on ASFA deadlines and the best interests of the child, the social worker likely would recommend an alternative permanent placement for the child. A social worker exercises independent professional judgment about the needs of the child and family and the services to be provided. Nevertheless, the social worker is an employee of the government (or of the private agency under contract to the government), and will inevitably develop recommendations sensitive to the agency's policies. A social worker cannot represent the legal interests of a child, but can express opinions that are important in determining the child's best interests.

In every jurisdiction the judge is the ultimate decision-maker in at least two points of the case: at the trial, deciding whether neglect, abuse, or abandonment of the child occurred; and at the permanency hearing, deciding whether the child shall be returned home or shall be placed elsewhere under an alternative arrangement permitted by ASFA. Judges have an obligation to review the case plan and approve, or disapprove, the permanency goal for the child. In many states, judges have decisions to make about other aspects of a case: visitation, interim placements, education, medical care, and more. Some states, however, have placed limits on judicial decision-making and give those tasks to the foster care agency. See section II.A. of this Chapter.

Because of their separate obligations, in a courtroom each lawyer and each social worker can seem at odds with one another. The judge puts all of the courtroom testimony and evidence together to arrive at a decision that is in the best interests of the child.

Despite courtroom arguments, some of the most successful outcomes in foster care cases occur when lawyers and social workers are a team with agreed goals.

B. Summary of Court Process

Federal laws implemented by the states have shaped the following sequence in the legal development of a case.

1. Pre-court events

Not all cases come before the court, and cases that do come into court can have a life of up to six months without court involvement. During that period, the relationship between the foster care agency and parents usually is governed by an agency contract describing the responsibilities of the parents to seek and accept services and visit with their children, as well as the services that the agency will provide. The agency can obtain money from the federal government during this period to subsidize the services they are offering, as long as it is conducting business according to federal standards. At the end of one hundred eighty days (six months) however, if the agency wishes to continue claiming federal money for the case it must file a petition for court intervention, alleging that the child is neglected, abused, or abandoned. Otherwise, the agency must close the case or finance it entirely without federal money.

2. Pre-trial court intervention

When a petition is filed in court (usually prepared by a social worker and a government attorney), the court determines whether it has jurisdiction. Usually this determination is made in an initial court hearing during which the allegations against the parent are examined, and the government may be asked to show "probable cause" that neglect, abuse, or abandonment of the child occurred. Based on the documentary and testamentary evidence presented, the judge (or magistrate or hearing officer) decides whether the case should stay in the court system and proceed to trial or stipulation. If the court decides to take jurisdiction of the case, a decision is made about who will take care of the child in the interim. If a judge decides that it is "contrary to the welfare of the child" to return home, the judge issues what usually is called a "shelter care" order. The foster care agency may enter the case at this point, though if the parents had voluntarily put their child in foster care prior to the court hearing, the foster care agency would just continue its supervision.

While attorneys are developing the legal case, the child should be receiving social services of all kinds: physical and mental health, shelter, schooling, and so forth. The parents' receipt of services is not so straightforward. Although the parents' cooperation with social workers and other service providers is key to whether the child will be returned, any of these providers can also be witnesses against them. In some states, case law protects parents from having to divulge information pre-trial through drug tests and psychological reports. E.g. *Laurie S. v. Superior Ct.,* 31 Cal Rptr. 2d 506 (1994); *Fruh v. State Dept. of Health and Rehabilitative Services,* 430 So.2d 581 (Fla. 1983).

3. Adjudication and disposition

There can be considerable variation between states as to the time it takes for a case to come to trial, depending on whether the state has a "speedy trial" provision. If the case must be heard within a few weeks, there will be less time for the parties to develop evidence to defend or prosecute the case. In most states, the government must prove its case by a preponderance of the evidence. That is, more than fifty percent of the evidence must support the government's case. If neglect, abuse, or abandonment is found, a disposition either takes place immediately following the trial, or within a few weeks thereafter. A disposition at this stage is a decision about where the child shall live now, and what interim services shall be offered while evidence is examined more closely and the case moves toward a permanency decision. The disposition order lists conditions that attach to the interim living arrangement. These interim arrangements are distinguished from the permanent disposition that occurs at the end of the case. Here again, there is great procedural variation between states. (Note, for example, the differences in whether an interim disposition order can be appealed, discussed in Subsection II.C of this chapter.) If the child has ties to a Native American tribe, other procedures apply as discussed in Chapter One, II.H and in Chapter Three, II.D.3.

4. Status hearings and reviews

ASFA has imposed an approximate one-year time period within which final decisions must be made for children who are removed from their families. During this interim period, the court is required to continue monitoring the case. Some of the greatest tensions occur between the court and the foster care agency during this interim period, for often each would like to direct where the child lives, what services are offered, and how resources are allocated.

5. The permanency hearing

Just prior to, or at, the twelve-month mark, final decisions are made by the court about whether the child shall be returned home, adopted, or placed under permanent guardianship (preferably with kin), or (if a teenager) permitted to live independently. These momentous decisions are to be made with full consideration of the foster care agency's recommendations, and of course with whatever mitigating evidence the parents may offer. The judge must give written reasons for the decision that include why there may be departures from the agency's recommendation. In many states this order is final and can be appealed. See Subsection II C of this chapter for a discussion of appeals.

6. Termination of parental rights hearing

If the court's decision is that the child should be adopted, the parents' rights must be formally terminated. There is great variation in how states proceed with this step. In some states, the same judge that has heard all of the evidence from the beginning of the court case also presides at the termination of parental rights (TPR) hearing. In other states, the TPR hearing is a new trial with a different judge than the one that heard the underlying neglect-abuse case. The elements to be proved are different than those in a neglect-abuse hearing. The U.S. Constitution extends many protections for parents to raise their children and those rights can only be terminated upon clear and convincing evidence. *Santosky v. Kramer*, 455 U.S. 745 (1982). Termination decisions can be appealed.

7. Post-decision reporting

All cases do not wrap up neatly at the final disposition or termination of parental rights stage. Sometimes children are returned home but enough uncertainty remains about their safety that the social services agency continues to monitor their condition. Or it may happen that the paperwork or negotiations are incomplete for subsidized guardianship or adoption. The judge may ask for reports to be submitted with the option of reopening the case. Older children who receive some subsidies between the ages of eighteen and twenty-one while they pursue education or job training may continue to be monitored in court reviews. If the case still qualifies as a foster care case, federal law requires that there be an administrative hearing every six months and an annual court review.

C. Summary of Administrative Reviews

Under the terms of the federal grant of money through Title VI of the Social Security Act that includes ASFA, every state must have a system for reviewing foster care cases. At a minimum, each case is to be reviewed "no less frequently than once every six months by either a court or by administrative review...." 42 U.S.C. § 675(5)(B).

States have interpreted this requirement in various ways. For example, in some states there is a court review at least every year and an administrative review every six months. In other states, there is a court review at least every six months for new cases or those involving young children, and in addition there is an administrative review every six months.

How does an administrative review differ from a court review? The federal statute defines administrative review as one:

> ...open to the participation of the parents of the child, conducted by a panel of appropriate persons at least one of whom is not responsible for the case management of, or the delivery of services to, either the child or the parents who are the subject of the review. 42 U.S.C. §675(6); ASFA §475(6)

Nothing is said about whether the child should be present. The parents' participation is voluntary, unless required by state law or court rules. The federal law does not even require the social workers who are involved with the family to be present. There is a list of matters to be considered at the review, however:

- safety of the child;
- continuing necessity for and appropriateness of the placement;
- extent of compliance with the case plan;
- extent of progress made towards alleviating or mitigating the causes necessitating placement in foster care; and
- likely date by which the child may be returned to and safely maintained in the home, or placed for adoption or legal guardianship, 42 U.S.C. §675(5)(B); ASFA §475(5)(B).

Administrative reviews are usually held away from court, often at the foster care agency. Because they are not in a courtroom and there is no judge presiding they tend to be much more informal than a court hearing. Some states look on administrative reviews as occasions to bring the whole family together and any other interested persons to air issues and problems. In other states, an administrative review is a critique of the social worker's performance. A critical event that should occur is review of the permanency goal. Questions that should be raised include whether participants should be working toward return of the child to his parents or whether it looks as if that strategy is failing and the realistic goal should be adoption, guardianship, or independent living.

While administrative reviews can be used to good effect to move cases along and protect the child, many states have not made administrative reviews and court proceedings work well together. Any major change in the permanency goal in an administrative review would have to be reviewed by a judge and supported by a court order. Attorneys and child advocates point out that in some states there can be a huge gap of time between an administrative review's goal change and a judge's review. For instance, if a judge reviews a case on January 2 and approves a goal of reunification, there is a subsequent administrative review on July 1 that changes the recommended goal to adoption, and the next court hearing is the permanency hearing set for December 15, all of the social service energy and skills would have been devoted for five-and-a-half months to achieving adoption rather than return home. The judge is then left with an accomplished fact: how can he order the child to return home when there has not been sufficient work with the parents to prepare the home? When the goal was changed administratively on July 1 the parents might have been left without a final order to appeal until the court hearing. Most states have an administrative appeal process, but often it is a system serving the entire government, rather than just the interests of the parties to family and juvenile cases, so the parents might fail to identify it as a resource. Such administrative appeals would address abuses within the system, for example, a failure to provide transportation for a disabled child. Most parties in a neglect-abuse case simply wait until a court hearing to raise the administrative issue with the judge. However, in states where a judge lacks power to order services after the adjudication, pursuing an administrative appeal could be a useful strategy.

D. A Typical Court Case

Calendar

Month

1   Removal of two children to kin, and infant to a foster home
1   Shelter care hearing (ASFA 12-month clock begins)
2   Adjudication of neglect
3   Disposition: all three children remain in placements
4   First administrative hearing: infant's goal changed to adoption
$4\frac{1}{2}$ First court review: court approves infant's adoption goal

A mother, Janice Jones, has three children: Johnny, 15 years old; Billy, 10 years old; and Tina, 3 months. Harry Smith, the father of Tina, has been living in the household. The father of Johnny and Billy is in prison. The police break up a domestic dispute between Ms. Jones and Mr. Smith, and in the process the children are removed from the home by a social worker.

The case is heard in court the next day. Separate counsel are assigned to Ms. Jones and Mr. Smith and to the children as a group. The judge finds that it would be "contrary to the welfare of the children" (ASFA language) to return the children home because there is probable cause to believe that there has been neglect of the children, and possibly abuse of them, as well as domestic violence toward the mother.

The case is prepared for trial quickly because this state has both a speedy trial provision and a fast-track schedule for decisions for little children. (In states that do not schedule trial quickly, there can be many weeks of "discovery"—that is, the pre-trial search for evidence in documents and from witnesses — and motions, such as requests to the court to postpone the trial or to force opposing counsel to produce documents.). Johnny and Billy are "placed" with their paternal grandparents and Tina is placed with foster parents who also are prospective pre-adoptive parents. While lawyers gather evidence in the case, the children's needs are assessed and, under pressure from the judge and the children's attorney, they begin to be addressed. A visitation schedule is set up for the parents.

The case comes to trial with evidence that Mr. Smith and Ms. Jones have been reported many times to the police and social services agency for domestic violence. The baby's health screen shows a "failure to thrive." Teachers report that the boys' school attendance has been very irregular. The judge finds neglect, but accepts evidence produced by Ms. Jone's lawyer that there has been no actual abuse of the children. The judge orders the children to remain in their current placements until a disposition hearing in one month. Meanwhile, Ms. Jones and Mr. Smith are ordered to submit to drug tests three times a week and to undergo psychological screenings. Mr. Smith is ordered to stay away from the home. The parents are also ordered to visit the children regularly and to cooperate with the social workers.

At disposition one month later, Mr. Smith's drug tests have all been positive for methamphetamine and a variety of other substances. Ms. Jones has skipped her drug tests. While Ms. Jones has visited her sons, no one has visited Tina. The judge's disposition order states that the children shall remain in their current placements while reunification services are offered to the family. The goal in the case plan will be family reunification, but on the recommendation of the social worker, there will be concurrent efforts to develop an adoption opportunity for the baby. Mr. Smith and Ms. Jones are ordered to continue drug tests, enter drug treatment, and continue visits with the children.

Four months into the one-year period prescribed by ASFA that began when the judge's first order was issued, the first administrative review is held. It is presided over by an administrative reviewer who is a state employee, but who has no other involvement in the case. Notice is sent to the parents, the grandparents, the foster parents, and the attorneys. Johnny and Billy are invited to come as well. Of those invited, all come except Mr. Smith, his attorney and the paternal grandfather. The social worker is there. The participants are seated around a table in a conference room at the foster care agency. The environment is conducive to free discussion. The dominant subject is Tina. The question before the group is whether the goal for her should be adoption, in that the parents have not visited. Despite vigorous protests by Ms. Jones and her attorney, the reviewer approves the social services' recommendation for adoption.

After the administrative review, at the next scheduled court review two weeks later, the social worker submits a report to the judge and parties stating that there has been no visitation with Tina. The foster parents would like to adopt her. The recommendation is for a TPR petition be filed immediately as to Tina and heard within two months, as permitted in the state's fast-track laws. The judge agrees. Tina then begins to move through a separate process from her brothers.

Ms. Jones continues to visit with her sons, though irregularly. She completes a one month detoxification program and begins a course of daytime drug treatment. Six months into the ASFA year, the parental rights of Ms. Jones and Mr. Smith are terminated as to Tina. An adoption petition is immediately filed. Ten months into the ASFA year another administrative review is held. The topics are whether adoption should be approved for Johnny and Billy and, alternatively, whether Johnny can move out of his grandparents' home as he wishes into an independent living arrangement. The children's lawyer and Ms. Jones, resist changing the goal to adoption, arguing that the boys are close to their mother and grandparents, and continued contact within the family is desirable. Inquiries are made about the grandparents' financial situation, and the goal is changed from family reunification to subsidized guardianship.

At the permanency hearing eleven months into the ASFA year, Ms. Jones' treatment advocate reports that she cannot tell at this point whether Ms. Jones will eventually achieve sobriety. The judge expresses that the children cannot be assuredly safe if they return home to Ms. Jones. The grandparents are willing to become guardians if they receive some financial assistance. Fortunately, subsidized guardianship is available in this state.

The outcome of the case is that Ms. Jones and Mr. Smith have their parental rights terminated as to Tina. Tina is adopted by the foster parents. The boys remain with their grandparents who now have the authority to make parental-type decisions for them. Visitation with their mother remains a possibility, to the satisfaction of all.

II. Significant Legal Issues Relating to Court Process

A. Extent of Judicial Power

A main tension in many states is whether the judge or the social service agency will have control over the details and likely, therefore, the outcome of the case. Some states assign a powerful role to the judge, who can (and in some states must) become involved in such social service details of the case as where the child shall be placed and how visitation shall be arranged. By contrast, in some other states courts of appeal or legislatures have firmly assigned those kinds of details to the social service agency, especially after the post-trial disposition.

1. Jurisdiction

Once a petition alleging child neglect, abuse, or abandonment has been submitted to the court, the judge has jurisdiction over the child. (Initially it is only to decide whether it is probable the allegations are true, giving a basis for continued jurisdiction). If the case continues past the initial hearing and the parents do not cooperate with court orders, they can be prevented from seeing their child and ultimately their parental rights can be terminated. Jurisdiction over the child is the true power the court has over the parents. In this civil law proceeding, the court can order the parents to participate in drug testing, psychological exams, visitation, and so forth, but if the parents refuse to follow the order the court cannot force them. Although the court has the power under civil laws to jail persons who are in contempt of court orders, that seldom happens because incarceration would not create the desired result. Jail is not a place where people become good parents.[26] A main point of the proceeding, after all, is to give the parents a chance to prove—or disprove—that they can nurture their child and provide a safe home.

The true perpetrator of wrongdoing to the child often is not a parent. It may be a boyfriend of the mother's, a cousin, or a neighbor. If the perpetrator lives in the household, the judge can insist that the mother separate herself from him, and that he be barred from the child. If he does not live in the household, the civil judge has no real power over him. He may be referred to criminal court, but in the meantime someone must be identified as having neglected, abused, or abandoned the child in order for the civil court to sustain its jurisdiction over the case and bring services to the child. In that situation, the wrongdoer often is identified as the mother on the theory that she failed to protect her child from harm. Advocates for victims of domestic violence strongly object to using the mother as a "straw man" for the real offender. *Nicholson v. Scoppetta,*344 F 3d 154 (2nd Cir. 2003). See also Cindy Lederman *et al., The Nexus Between Child Maltreatment and Domestic Violence,* 2 J. Center for Families, Child & Courts 129 (2000).

A court's jurisdiction over a case lasts until the judge dismisses it, or until the child "ages out," usually between eighteen and twenty-one years. ASFA puts strong pressure on courts to resolve cases within one year, but jurisdiction does not automatically lapse at the end of a year. It lasts until a judge determines that the main issues have been resolved and the child is now safe.

2. Placement

A frequent tug of war between a judge and a foster care agency occurs over where a child shall live after she has been removed from her parents. In some states that issue would appear to be settled by the legislature which has assigned placement power to either the judge or the foster care agency. For example, New York's Family Court Act, §225, Art. 10, Part 5, § 1055 (a) states:

> The Court may place the child in the custody of a relative or other suitable person, or of the Commission of Social Services or of such other officer, board or department as may be authorized to receive children as public charges, or a duly authorized association, agency, society or in an institution suitable for the placement of the child.

Virginia (Code of Virginia, 16.1-278,2), Georgia (Official Code of Georgia, 49-5-3(12)(D)), and Idaho (General laws of Idaho 16.1602) laws state, to the contrary, that placement authority is with the agency. That is not the end of the struggle, however. For example, in Virginia, although the law states in one place, "The board or public agency that places the child shall have final authority to determine the appropriate placement for the child," (16.1-278.2) in another place it gives the court the power to review and make changes to the foster care plan, which of course includes placement. (16.1-281.C1)

In some states power to choose the placement has been decided by case law. Rhode Island (*In re Doe*, 390 A. 2d 390 (RI 1978) and Vermont (*In re G.F.* 455 A. 2d 805 (VT 1982) hand decision-making authority to the agency. So does Massachusetts, which says the agency "has virtually free rein to place that child in a foster home of its choosing" when it has permanent custody of a child—but then notes that this placement is subject to court review every six months. *Care and Protection of Three Minors*, 467 N.E. 2d 851, 861 (Mass 1984)).

A well-phrased explanation of the need for both the court and the agency to examine placements is given in *Application of Sammy P.*, 503 N.Y.S. 2d 243 (Fam. Ct. 1986):

> The Court certainly agrees that foster care agencies must have wide discretion to deal with children placed in their care. Certainly it is neither feasible nor desirable for the court to become a supervisor in the day to day operations of the agency. However, the foster placement at which a child resides is at the very heart of the treatment plan. It determines such things as the limitation on the child's freedom, the type of children with whom he will live, and the level of care he will receive.....
> [C]ommon sense, a plain reading of the statute, and its legislative history strongly suggest that the Court has jurisdiction to consider whether a facility or place where a foster child resides furthers the child's best interests and the express state policy requiring permanency planning.

In every state the placement struggle is likely to have been addressed in statutes, court rules, or case law. The federal government has entered the argument as well. The final HHS rule for its ASFA regulations states that federal payments would be denied if placements were made by the judge, rather than the agency. 45 C.F.R. §1356(g)(3). Later that stance was eased through an HHS interpretation that the judge must consider the recommendation of the agency before making a decision. [27] It seems that there is never a last word on the subject.

3. Visitation

The struggle between the court and the foster care agency over who shall determine the schedule and conditions of visitation is analyzed in the same way as placement problems: through state statutes, court rules, and case law.

Sometimes the judge has the power to make visitation arrangements, but declines to exercise it. In *In re Adoption of Galvin*, 773 N.E. 2d 1007 (Mass.App.Ct. 2002), the court of appeals sternly corrected a trial court that would not exercise its power: it said the judge, not the social service agency, was required by statute to consider whether sibling visitation should occur, decide how it should be implemented, oversee the arrangements, evaluate the effectiveness and appropriateness of it, and make modifications as circumstances change. The Maryland Court of Appeals remanded a case where the judge did not acknowledge responsibility to address visitation arrangements. *In re Caya B.*, 834 A.2d 997 (Md. App. 2003). It is the judge who must make visitation decisions according to The Revised Code of Washington, 13.34.130, and the District of Columbia Code §16-2310(d), explicitly place visitation decisions in the judge's hands, while it is likely that states that award placement power to the foster care agency would also tend to leave details about visitation to the agency.

In California, where the judge controls visitation, a series of cases decided which groups or individuals could also have a say in how and whether visitation should occur. Therapists from private agencies were excluded from making the final decision, because the judge lacked jurisdiction over them. *In re Donnovan J.*, 68 Cal Rptr. 714 (Cal.Ct.App. 1997). Children were also excluded from those who could veto visitation on the theory that they lacked maturity to make such an important decision. *In re Julie M.*, 81 Cal Rptr. 2d. 354 (Cal.Ct.App.1999). (The California cases are considered in greater detail in Chapter Three, II.A., and in Edwards, *Judicial Oversight of Parental Visitation in Family Reunification Cases*, 54 Juvenile and Family Court Journal 1 (Summer 2003)).

4. Services

The question of when and how services are provided can test a court's jurisdictional limits. Once it has been decided that a committed child needs treatment, under which circumstances can a judge order a state agency to provide that treatment? A few states have great flexibility to order any services a child may need. For example, the D.C. Code at Title 16-2320(a)(5) says:

> The Division [i.e. the court] may make such other disposition as is not prohibited by law and as the Division deems to be in the best interests of the child. The Division shall have authority to (i) order any public agency of the District of Columbia to provide any service the Division determines is needed and which is within the agency's legal authority, and (ii) order any private agency receiving public funds for services to families or children to provide any such services when the

Division deems it is in the best interests of the child and within the true scope of the legal obligations of the agency.

Also putting power in the hands of the judge are courts in the state of Utah, in *In re Tanner*, 549 P.2d 703 (Utah 1976): "...[W]hen there is some such serious neglect relating to basic necessities as to put the health and welfare of a minor in hazard, there must be some remedy...this is the special responsibility of the juvenile court."

When family or juvenile courts order agencies to expend funds which those agencies claim not to have, however, judges may find themselves reprimanded.

Rhode Island's *In re Doe*, 390 A.2d 390 (R.I. 1978) makes that point. The family court ordered the mental health agency to provide funds for treatment in a specific facility for a disturbed child. The agency said it had exhausted funds allocated for that purpose. The family court responded that the agency should draw on funds in a different part of its budget and held the agency's director in contempt. The Court of Appeals said the family court had no authority to review the agency's budget. The agency was better able "to allocate scarce resources among competing requirements." In accord is *In re Matter of L*, 546 P.2d 153 (Or.App. 1976)

B. Who May Enforce a Legal Right

Often a crowd of people enter a courtroom ready to testify to some aspect of the case. Sometimes there are arguments over who is a "party," who has "standing" to raise issues, who is permitted to participate in some capacity, and who is excluded. Neglect-abuse cases, of which foster care is one aspect, can be especially confusing in this regard because they function partly like criminal cases, in that the government is the initial petitioner, and partly like civil cases with multiple participants who have different interests.

If one examines legal vocabulary to find terms that describe the legal status of people in a neglect-abuse case, it is quickly apparent that the usual words do not fit this situation. For example, "party" is defined in Black's Law Dictionary (7th Ed., 1999) as "one by whom, or against whom, a lawsuit is brought." In the context of a foster care case, that would mean that only a government agency (usually the public foster care agency) and the alleged wrongdoer (usually a biological parent) would be parties. This definition leaves out the possibility for the child to take an active part in the proceeding, not to mention others who may have a real stake in the outcome. A better question may be: who among the crowd of people standing before the judge may enforce a legal right at the heart of a case? For example, foster care parents may not want a child removed from their home, or may want to adopt a foster child. The judge may, or may not, decide that this is a legal issue at the heart of the foster care case. If the judge decides that it is, she may permit the foster parents to argue their case, and even put on witnesses, and obtain documents. If the judge decides it is not an issue at the heart of the case, she may limit the foster parents to giving information that the court requests. Once the person and the legal right are identified, the important follow-up problem is whether the right actually can be enforced, that is, whether the person has adequate legal representation.

1. The government, representing the public foster care agency

The government is a party to a neglect-abuse case. It is in fact the petitioning party that initiates the case. A government's attorney represents every public agency involved with the child. When a child is in foster care, the public foster care agency is represented by the government attorney. Through its attorney, the foster care agency has full legal resources at its command. For example it can obtain documents, present witnesses, cross-examine the parents' and child's witnesses, and appeal unfavorable rulings.

A government's attorney does not directly represent the child. The government attorney represents the government agency that has responsibility for the child. Before the child enters foster care, she may be the responsibility of a state child protection agency. Then the government's attorney represents that agency. After the child enters foster care, she may be placed in a foster home managed by a private agency under contract to the public agency. Nevertheless, the government's attorney represents the government's foster care agency that retains oversight and monitoring functions of the private agency.

The social worker on a case is not a party to the case. She may appear as the government's witness, often its most important witness. (Social workers may also appear as a child's or parent's witness). A social worker from a private foster care agency may be called as a government's witness as well. When a child testifies in a case, it is often as a government's witness.

2. The biological parents

Parents have a constitutionally-protected right to raise their child free of government intervention, unless it can be proved that the child is, or imminently may be, harmed. *Meyer v. Nebraska,* 262 U.S. 390 (1923) (The word "liberty" includes the right of an individual to "establish a home and bring up children). *Pierce v. Society of Sisters,* 268 U.S. 510 (1924) (There is no "general power of the State to standardize its children"). *Stanley v. Illinois,* 405 U.S. 645 (1972)

(The court cannot refuse an unmarried father a hearing "when the issue at stake is the dismemberment of his family).

The biological parents are more fully armed with legal rights than any other participants in a neglect-abuse case. The constitutional assurance of due process for parents is explicit. Notice, the right to confront witnesses against one, and cross-examination are all available. (These are more fully discussed in Chapter Three, II.D). Nevertheless, there can be many barriers to actually exercising these rights. Local court rules may not permit an indigent parent to be represented at all stages of a proceeding. *Smith v. Marion Cty. Dept. of Welfare,* 635 N.E. 2d 1144 (Ind. 1994). While indigent parents may be assigned counsel, parents who are poor but have some income may not be able to afford counsel. The burden placed on judges by the U.S. Supreme Court in the *Lassiter* decision, 452 U.S. 18 (1981) (that is, to determine case-by-case whether indigent parents should have counsel at TPR hearings) may discourage them from appointing counsel. Parents' counsel may not be well-trained or skilled. All judges may not be aware of the extent of constitutional protections. Trials may be frowned upon and stipulated agreements encouraged. Parents' counsel may believe that ASFA encourages stipulated agreements rather than litigation. 42 U.S.C. §671(a)(15).

Unmarried fathers do not automatically have the same constellation of rights that mothers have. They must prove under a constitutional analysis that they had grasped the opportunity for fatherhood in some tangible way: for example, acknowledgement of paternity, visitation, or child support. *Lehr v. Robinson,* 463 U.S. 248 (1983). If they have, their parental rights cannot be terminated except by clear and convincing evidence. *Santosky v. Kramer,* 455 U.S. 745 (1982). But if they have not, beyond an initial notice, not much attention needs be paid to them. (Of course, state laws, including state constitutions, can establish due process protections that go beyond the federal constitutional standard).

While parents inarguably have rights to enforce in a foster care case—the right to raise their children, the right to due process of law if the children are removed—all of the elements mentioned are part of considering whether parents *actually* have the opportunity to fully assert their rights and defend themselves.

3. The child

The child is in a strange legal position in a foster care case. The case is *about* her. ASFA refers to the child's safety throughout, almost as if it were her right. Yet she is not explicitly accorded any legal right to safety. Nor may she choose to live, or not live, with her biological parents. There is a general sense in a foster care case that she is being defended, but often she is more a witness to her fate than an active litigant.

A number of people in a hearing may claim to speak for the child. These may include the government's attorney, the social worker, and perhaps a child advocate who could be either a guardian *ad litem*, Court Appointed Special Advocate (CASA), or an attorney. The primary client of several of these people is not the child, but rather their employer. For example, the primary client of the government's attorney is the public foster care agency (or other government entity, like the child protection agency.) It is only secondarily the child. The government's attorney often expresses society's outrage at the injury to the child and calls for the parent or other responsible adult to be held accountable. Of course, the government's attorney is required to advocate for services to the child that ameliorate her condition, ASFA, 42 U.S.C. §629b(7)(B), but which of those services is he likely to pursue actively? The answer usually is: those services recommended by the foster care agency that he represents. For example, if the foster care agency holds contracts with two residential treatment facilities, it is unlikely that the state's attorney would advocate for placement in a third noncontractual facility even if it were a better match for the child's needs.

Similarly, the social worker, though exercising independent professional judgment, must often refer to agency policies. She may advocate within the foster care agency for the most fitting services even if they must be found outside of usual providers, but in the courtroom the social worker's advocacy may be limited by what is available according to agency policy or funds.

Whether a child has independent legal representation in court, and thus the opportunity to be "heard" by the court, depends on state law and local court practice. Much has been made of a recent amendment to The Child Abuse Prevention and Treatment Act (CAPTA), that requires guardians *ad litem* and CASA to have appropriate training for their representation of a child in a neglect-abuse case. Keeping Children Safe Act of 2003, P.L. 108-36, amending CAPTA, P.L. 100-294; 42 U.S.C. §5106a(b)(2)(A)(ix). Only states that have accepted CAPTA funding (all but two have) must meet that standard. But even where a child's interests are represented, court rules may limit how fully a guardian *ad litem* or CASA may participate in obtaining documents and cross-examining witnesses, and even more fundamentally, how well trained they are in the law. If the child's representative is not a lawyer, the full range of legal strategies may not be at her command.

There is great variation between states as to when a child comes to court, and whether her opinions may be heard. Often, she is the only witness to the abuse. Unless court rules or cases permit examination in judge's chambers with only attorneys present (*In re Elizabeth T.,* 12 Cal.Rptr.2d 10 (1992); *In re Laura H.,* 11 Cal. Rptr.2d 285 (1992)) the child can be cross-examined by the lawyer for the very person who allegedly mistreated her. The alleged abuser need not take the stand to offer a defense, and therefore avoids cross-examination by the child's advocate. In some states, the child's advocate is not even expected to take an active part in the trial. Under those conditions, it stretches the mind to say that the child is a party with the same power and legal protections as the parent or government agency.

Maryland, like a number of other states, explicitly accords party status to a child. Maryland Courts and Judicial Proceedings, Article §3-801(u)(1)(i). *In re Adoption/Guardian T. No. 97036005*, 746 A.2d 379 (MD. 2000). In New York, a court said children "have a constitutionally-protected right to be free of arbitrary state decisions that have a significant impact on their custody and welfare." *In re Adoption of Jonee*, 695 N.Y.S. 2d 920 (Fam.Ct. 1999). In accord is *In re Adoption of Corey*, 707 N.Y.S.2d 767 (Fam. Ct. 1999). Those courts appear to be proposing that a child is not only a party, but one that has a "right to make a legal claim or seek judicial enforcement of a duty or right," in other words, one who has "standing," a term that refers to entitlements under constitutional law. Black's Law Dictionary (7th Ed., 1999). That would go far to make the child an equal in court with the alleged wrongdoer and the government.

4. The Foster Parents

Before ASFA, it was not unusual for children to be removed from foster parents suddenly on authority of a court order issued in a hearing of which the foster parents had no notice and no right to participate. Congress was determined to give foster parents an opportunity to participate in proceedings. Thus, ASFA contains a provision that foster parents (as well as preadoptive parents or relatives) must be "provided with notice of, and an opportunity to be heard in any review or hearing to be held with respect to the child…." 42 U.S.C. §675(5)(G). The statute goes on to clarify that this provision does not make a foster parent a "party," nor does it exclude the possibility. That decision is in the hands of the judge or subject to state statute or court rule.

There are no universal rules about how fully foster parents may participate in the legal proceedings under ASFA. Courts can decide differently whether foster parents may advance their own issues (for example, adoption of the foster child), cross-examine the social worker or parent, or obtain documents. Even where foster parents have not been designated "parties," some courts have given them great leeway to litigate. E.g. *Bowens v. Maynard*, 324 S.E. 2d 145 (W.Va. 1984). Foster parents were permitted into a TPR hearing in Massachusetts with counsel, even though the judge acknowledged they had no constitutional right to participate. The judge concluded the court would profit from their assistance. *Custody of a Minor*, 432 N.E. 2d 546 (Mass. 1982). *Smith v. O.F.F.E.R.* went so far as to say that foster parents could raise issues on be-half of children, although this holding was in the context of a federal class ac-tion regarding due process in foster care, rather than a situation involving neg-lect-abuse itself.

5. Other government agencies, private agencies and independent contractors

In addition to the public foster care agency, other government agencies (for example, one responsible for mental health matters), and private agencies (for example, residential treatment facilities), and independent contractors (for example, psychologists in private practice) appear in the courtroom from time to time. They are there to give advice, or to be witnesses or advocates for one of the parties or for a particular position. They are helping the judge reach an informed decision. Can these other groups be permitted to fully litigate issues in the case? Unless there is a state statute or court rule covering this situation, the degree and way in which they participate often depends on whether the judge finds that she has jurisdiction over them. Jurisdiction includes the power of the court to order an individual or entity to take actions relating to the case. The District of Columbia has a statute, D.C. Code §16-2320(a)(5), that per-mits the court to order any government agency to undertake any lawful task. Many neglect-abuse courts do not have similar authority, and thus are lim-ited to ordering the social service agency to accomplish tasks through its con-tracts and memoranda of understanding. In *In re Donnovan J.,* 68 Cal.Rptr.2d 714 (Cal.Ct.App.1997), the judge would not permit a private therapist to de-cide whether or not a child and parent could visit, because the juvenile court had no direct jurisdiction over the therapist.

C. Timing of Appeals

Timing can be everything in protection of rights. That is why the ability to ap-peal an order may be decisive for a parent or child. For example, if a judge de-cides at the disposition after trial that an infant will be placed with a foster fam-ily, and if a parent is not permitted to appeal that decision alleging errors that occurred at trial, a year or even more may go by until appeal is permitted. Dur-ing that time, the infant may bond with the foster family, persuading the social worker and psychologist to recommend that she be adopted by the foster par-ents, because removing her from the only family she knows would be harmful.

State laws differ greatly regarding which orders are "final" and suitable for appeal. Some states permit appeal at every stage of a case where the goal for the family changes, for example, from "family reunification" to "adoption." Such a change might occur at an initial disposition (for example, a child who was returned home at the shelter care hearing might be placed in foster care at the disposition after the trial), at a review hearing, and at the permanency hearing.[28] Indeed, in D.C., a child (but not a parent) may take an interlocutory appeal from the first placement order, as well as any other, and it must be heard on an emergency schedule. D.C. Code §16-2328 (Interlocutory means prior to a final order). Opposing this philosophy are those states that adhere to a "one final order" rule, meaning that a party may appeal only once at the end of the process. The end might be a TPR action. It is apparent that by the time a case reaches the TPR stage, so much has been in place for so long that the case would no longer be about whether there was originally neglect or abuse, but rather about what would be best for the children given their current situation.

The court in *In re Murray*, 556 NE 2d 1169, 1172-1173 (Ohio 1990), described why it is important to give early opportunities for appeal:

> There is no requirement that the agency having custody of the child be required to seek permanent custody. If the agency fails to seek permanent custody and the temporary order remains in effect, the parent is without a remedy to attempt to demonstrate errors in the initial juvenile proceedings which resulted in the loss of custody. Even if the court eventually terminates the temporary custody order and returns the child to his or her parents…the initial determination neglect or dependency will not then be in issue.

III. Conclusion

There is nothing simple about litigating a neglect-abuse case. In addition to all of the human complexities arising in troubled family systems, there are layers of laws, ranging from cases under the U.S. Constitution, multiple federal statutes and the cases interpreting them, state statutes that incorporate federal mandates but also express state policies, and the cases that interpret them. In addition there are clashes of culture among practitioners of various professions that express opinions, such as psychologists, physicians, social workers, teachers, and drug treatment specialists. Moreover there are ambiguities in the system: who speaks for the child? Since it is the state, and not the child, who is the moving party, how can the child's interests best be presented? Although the action is in civil law, does it not also partake of criminal law in that it punishes the parents and argues mistreatment of a child as an offense against society? How fully may foster parents participate in a case? Must the parents be witnesses against themselves by yielding pre-trial evidence of impairment through psychological exams and drug tests?

The confusion and complexity offer many litigation opportunities for the conscientious advocate. While neglect-abuse cases often roll through the system as if only state law and local court rules apply, the educated advocate can reach into constitutional law, mine the rights and responsibilities inherent in federal statutes like Medicaid and The Americans with Disabilities Act, and make a great difference in the outcome of the case. An advocate can vigorously represent a party to the case, while still being a responsible team member, using a heightened knowledge of federal and state law, child development milestones, and substance abuse treatment to negotiate outcomes that will serve the entire family system.

APPENDIX A

LIABILITY

I. Introduction

It is unfortunate that sometimes things go wrong—a foster parent molests a foster child, a foster child steals a car and causes an accident. The possibility that a foster parent or a foster care agency will get sued is a constant reality. Just the threat of lawsuits affects the policies and practices of all agencies. All social workers and those who are responsible for agency operations need to know the basic elements of liability.

The best protections against liability are adherence to the laws and practices that result in good foster care and early detection of situations that can lead to liability. The earlier the agency is aware of a potential liability, the sooner steps can be taken to minimize damage and perhaps even avoid a lawsuit. Potential liability should be brought to the attention of legal counsel as quickly as possible. Therefore, social workers and agency administrators need to have in place a system that requires reporting and documentation of incidents and circumstances that call for further investigation. By responding appropriately, agencies not only solve the immediate problem but also improve their practices.

Foster parents and agency employees might resist documenting and reporting potential liability because no one wants to overreact to situations and no one wants to be either the object or source of criticism. There is a tendency to keep errors hidden. This is a mistake. Covering up is far worse than the consequences of error. Not only can injuries be exacerbated but insurance coverage can be affected by the discovery and reporting of circumstances that result in liability.

There is no such thing as a comprehensive explanation of liability because the outcome of each case depends on the facts of the incident at issue and the laws and regulations of the jurisdiction where it occurred. In other words, liability is state-law specific and fact sensitive. Moreover, liability law is affected by state and federal court decisions and new decisions are issued with some frequency. This Appendix offers an introduction to the most important issues regarding liability and contains references to cases and commentary for further research. The Selected Bibliography and Resources Appendix provides additional resources.

An examination of liability begins with a careful reading of state laws pertaining to foster care and the liability of private and public agencies that provide child welfare and foster care services. Next, one should read state court decisions that have dealt with liability in the context of foster care or agency relations with children. While reported cases can be helpful in describing how liability issues are viewed by courts in a particular state or federal court, they do not tell the whole story. Many lawsuits do not result in trials or in decisions that are published. Many suits are dropped or settled "out of court." Sometimes decisions are not appealed. For attorneys seriously engaged in prosecuting or defending liability suits, it may be cost-effective to use a legal research service that collects and reports trial court and jury trial results. These services can reveal the circumstances that result in successful liability suits and the cost of such suits to agencies and individuals. (E.g. National Association of State Jury Verdict Publishers. www.juryverdicts.com).

II. Foster Parent Liability

A. Overview

Liability affects foster parents in several ways. Foster parents are legally obligated to properly care for children in a manner that does not subject them to danger or injury. In legal terms, they must adhere to a "standard of care." If foster parents act in a manner that falls below the standard of care they would be acting negligently. If this negligence causes injury, it must then be asked if the foster parent is legally liable to the foster child. In addition to suits based on negligence, foster parents can also be liable for intentional injuries that they cause and for criminal acts that harm their foster children. For example, foster parents are liable when they assault or sexually molest a foster child. Foster parents can be sued when a foster child is injured and they can be sued if a foster child injures someone or damages property. Liability issues may also arise if a foster parent or a family member is injured by a foster child. This Section discusses foster parent immunity from suit, insurance and indemnification, and foster parents' liability for the acts of foster children. Covered in other Sections of this Appendix are such issues as the relationship of the foster parent to the agency, whether the agency is legally liable for the acts of the foster parent (III. B.) and foster parent liability under 42 U.S.C. §1983, the federal civil rights law. (IV.F.)

B. Can Foster Parents be Sued?

While mowing the lawn the foster parent negligently injures the foster child. There is no insurance for this incident. If the parent had injured a neighbor (or the neighbor's child), there is little doubt that the foster parent would be held responsible for such injuries. It would seem logical that a foster child should be able to sue the foster parent. However, it is not this clear. Usually children cannot sue their biological parents even if they were injured by the negligence of their parents. This principle is known as "parental immunity." Should foster children be treated like biological children when injured as result of the foster parent's negligence? Or should foster children be treated differently? If a biological parent would be immune from suit should a foster parent in a similar situation also be immune from being sued by a foster child? Foster parent immunity from suit must be ascertained by looking at the laws of the particular state. Sometimes foster parents are protected by the same immunity provided to biological parents. *Nichol v. Stass,* 735 N.E. 2d 582 (Ill. 2000). (Foster parents are entitled to judicially created parental immunity the same as biological parents); *Brown v. Phillips,* 342 S.E. 2d 786 (Ga. Ct. App. 1986) (Because foster parents act in place of the parents, they are immune from suit absent evidence willful or malicious action).

Sometimes a state will enact legislation that spells out when and under what circumstances foster parents are immune. *Spikes v. Banks,* 586 N.W.2d 106 (MI. Ct. App. 1998), involved the application of a state statue (MCL 722.163(1); MSA 25.358(63(1)) creating immunity for foster parents that stated:

> A foster child may maintain an action against his or her foster parent
> ... for injuries suffered as a result of the alleged ordinary negligence
> of the foster parent... except in either of the following instances:
> - (a) If the alleged negligent act involves an exercise of reasonable
>   parental authority over the child.
> - (b) If the alleged negligent act involves an exercise of reasonable
>   parental discretion with respect to the provision of food, cloth-
>   ing, housing, medical and dental services and other care.

In *Spikes* the foster mother had permitted her adult nephew to reside in her home along with at least one minor female. The minor female had sexual relations with the nephew. The foster mother knew that the nephew had serious criminal charges pending because the police had come to the house looking for him. The charges included "first-degree criminal sexual conduct." The court ruled she was not immune under the statute because immunity is not warranted "in circumstances involving the sexual abuse of a minor when the caregiver knew or should have known of the abuse and did nothing to prevent it." Whether or not foster parents would be treated the same as biological (or adoptive) parents if there were legislative changes to the common law of parental immunity from suits by their children or for damages caused by children would depend upon the actual language of the statute and judicial interpretation of ambiguous language.[29]

Wisconsin has enacted a comprehensive law that provides immunity to foster parents, foster children, and foster care agencies, and provides exceptions to that immunity. (Wis. Stat. Ann. 895.485) The commentary states that the law:

> [c]reates standards for determining liability of foster parents and agencies. It provides that, except as provided in the statutes relating to the use of fireworks and automobile insurance coverage, a foster parent is immune from civil liability for:(a) any act or omission of the foster parent while acting in his or her capacity as a foster parent; and (b) any act or omission of a foster child in the foster parent's care. However the immunity will not apply if an act or omission of a foster parent was not done in good faith or was not in compliance with specific written instructions that are provided by the agency that placed the child. The good faith of, and compliance with written instructions by, a foster parent will be presumed in any civil action.[30]

As foster parents obtain more authority over children they have greater reason to claim the protections of parental immunity and greater reason to argue that they ought to have the same legal protections as biological parents. Moreover, it is reasonable to assume that imposing liability on foster parents, especially when biological parents would be immune, would discourage people from becoming foster parents. On the other hand, restricting the ability of a foster child to recover for damages inflicted by foster parents is questionable social policy since it was the government that placed the child into foster care. The answer lies in the legislative examples discussed here—a predictable system that protects both foster children and foster parents by providing immunity or imposing liability as warranted by the facts.

C. Indemnification and Insurance for Foster Parents

It is possible to envision a system in which the foster parent would trade immunity for indemnification[31] from the agency. Any actual damages awarded to the injured foster child could either be paid by the agency or from insurance purchased by the foster parent individually or from a state-sponsored program. It is important to note that when foster parents are not immune from suit they might be state or agency employees for indemnification or insurance purposes. States can if they wish indemnify foster parents for the damages that foster parents may be forced to pay because of their negligence.[32] For example, Arizona requires prior permission if a foster child will be participating in certain "activities and functions." This statute provides that "[t]he state shall indemnify and hold harmless the agency or foster parents for liability that may be incurred or alleged as a result of giving such permission, when such permission is reasonably and prudently given. The state shall provide the defense of any action alleging such liability." (Arizona Rev. Stat. Ann. 8-513). Illinois however, explicitly includes "individuals who serve as foster parents" as employees for purposes of indemnification. Ill. Comp. State Ann 350/1(b) (West 1997).[33] Some states like Iowa have created "foster home insurance funds." Iowa Code Annotated Title VI-Subtitle 6 §237.13(3) provides that the Iowa fund "shall pay, on behalf of each licensed foster home, any valid and approved claim of foster children, their parents, guardian or guardians ad litem for damages arising from the foster care relationship and the provision of foster care services. The fund shall also reimburse licensed foster homes for property damage or bodily injury, as a result of the activities of the foster child, and reasonable and necessary legal fees incurred in defense of civil claims filed [against the fund] and any judgments awarded as a result of such claims." The fund does not cover a "loss arising out of a foster parent's lascivious acts, indecent contact, or sexual activity" (as defined elsewhere in Iowa law). §327.13(4.d). In addition, the fund does not cover "the liability of a foster parent due solely to the foster parent's failure to obtain automobile or homeowners insurance". §237.13(4.h).[34]

D. Homeowners Insurance and Injuries to Foster Children

Especially in states that do not provide for indemnification or state-sponsored insurance, foster parents and private agencies are always seeking ways to protect themselves against the costs of injuries to or caused by foster children. Usually foster parents are required to have homeowners insurance with the expectation that this form of insurance will cover at least some of the losses that can occur. However, it is far from clear whether homeowners insurance will respond to injuries to or caused by a foster child. There is very little reported case law in this area. One case is *National Union Fire Ins. Co. of Pittsburgh v. Lynette C.*, 279 Cal. Rptr. 394 (Cal. App. 3 Dist. 1991). In this case an insurance company paid a judgment to the biological parents of a foster child when it was found that the foster mother did not protect the child from the foster father, who sexually molested her. Even though the molestation was an intentional criminal act of the foster father, the foster mother's failure to protect the foster child was negligent and the negligent acts of the foster parents were covered by the insurance policy.

Whether or not a foster child is a "resident" for insurance coverage purposes was addressed in *In Risk Management Div. General Services Dep't of State ex rel. Apodaca v. Farmers Ins. Co. of Arizona,* 75 P.3d 404 (N.M. App. 2003), where a foster child drowned in a toilet.[35] The foster child's biological mother sued the foster parents, who looked to their homeowners insurance for coverage.[36] The insurance company argued that the foster child was a household resident and, because the policy does not provide coverage for injury to or death of residents, the claim for the death of the foster child was not covered. The court did not decide the issue but sent the case back to the trial court for additional fact-finding. The opinion reviews cases from around the country on this issue and concludes that whether a foster child is a "resident" would depend on the specific facts of the situation. Such facts would include the actual or intended duration of the child's stay in the home and the subjective relationship of the child to the foster parents. The court also stated

> [t]hat an insurer cannot have it both ways. For example, if the foster child is not considered a resident for purposes of coverage for tortious acts on third parties, the child cannot, then, be considered a resident for purposes of exclusion. (Citation omitted).

E. Liability of Foster Parents for Acts of the Foster Child

A parent is not usually vicariously liable[37] for the intentional acts of a child simply on the basis of his or her status as a parent of the child. However, there are exceptions to this general principle. The parent could be liable if there was a principle-agent relationship between the parent and child, if the parent ratified, encouraged, or directed the acts of the child, or if the child's acts were the result of a "dangerous tendency" known to the parent. There are states that have by statute made parents liable for the intentional acts of their children. As with laws that protect parents from being sued by their own children, the question here is whether or not foster parents will be treated like biological parents. Are foster parents similarly liable? In *Kerins v. Lima,* 680 N.E. 2d 32 (Mass. 1997) the court ruled that when a foster child sets fire to a building the foster parents are not liable and that there are strong policy reasons for not holding foster parents liable for acts of foster children.[38]

F. Conclusion

As ought to be obvious by now the issues surrounding the liability of foster parents to foster children are complicated and sensitive to state laws. The same is true of injuries by foster children to foster parents and others. Among the questions that must be asked are:

Was the injury to the foster child caused by a foster parent's intentional or criminal act?

Is the foster parent immune from being sued?

What is the legal relationship of the foster parent to the agency?

Is the agency responsible for the acts of the foster parents?

Is there any insurance?

Is the foster parent entitled to indemnification from the agency or government?

If the foster child caused an injury, is the foster parent responsible for the actions of the foster child?

III. Public Foster Care Agency Liability

A. Overview

Issues concerning the legal liability of public foster care agencies can be complex and even confusing. This section provides an introduction to the liability of foster care agencies and the major issues that affect it. Many of the issues are identical or similar to the liability issues faced by private foster care agencies which are addressed in Section V of this Appendix.

Public foster care agencies have a legal obligation to protect foster children from harm. If this obligation to care for and protect foster children and to act in accordance with the accepted standard of care is violated, and a child, a foster parent, or someone else is injured, the agency will be liable. That is, the agency will be legally responsible for the damages caused by the injury. This violation of the duty to act properly and in accordance with applicable laws, standards and principles is called negligence.[39] Agency officials, administrators and social workers are supposed to abide by applicable laws and regulations, act competently, and avoid practices and behaviors that are incompatible with accepted practices and standards pertaining to the operation of a foster care system. Whether or not an agency will be found liable will turn on whether the agency's actions or failure to act fall below the standard of care that is required of a child welfare agency caring for children in foster care.

Standards of care can be established by state statute[40], regulations, policies and practices, and by national professional organizations that publish standards for foster care or social work such as the American Council on Accreditation, the National Association of Social Workers, the Child Welfare League of America, and the American Public Human Services Association.[41]

Deshaney v. Winnebago County Department of Social Services, 489 U.S. 189 (1989), is a United States Supreme Court case that dealt with the liability of public child welfare agencies. In *Deshaney,* a child had been removed from his family by a local child welfare agency. The agency evaluated the family and decided to return the child to his father's care. After the child was returned he was seriously and intentionally injured by the father. Although *Deshaney* is not a foster care case it is required reading because the U.S. Supreme Court attempts to identify the people to whom the agency will owe a "duty of care". While the Supreme Court has not yet decided a case where the child was injured while in foster care, the cases in the lower courts leave no doubt that once a child is placed into foster care, the state is responsible for the care of the child and can be legally liable for injuries to or caused by foster children.[42]

B. Is the Agency Liable for the Actions of the Foster Parents?

There is a legal term known as "respondeat superior". This is a legal principle that means that someone in a position of authority (an employer) is responsible for the acts of those subject to that authority (the employee). For instance, can agency can be liable if it or its agents or employees were negligent? An agency might well be responsible for its employees' negligence but not for its foster parents' negligence. For example, if a foster parent strikes and injures a foster child, the agency might not be liable for the actual striking of the child by the foster parent But if it were proven that the agency knew that this foster parent had struck this or another foster child and the agency nonetheless took no action, the agency could be found to be negligent for allowing the child to be cared for by the foster parents.

It can be difficult to discern which foster parent acts can cause agency liability. There are several factors to be considered. The two most important are state law and the precise nature of the foster parent-agency relationship. For example, an employer-employee relationship can, depending on state law, enable the acts of the foster parent to be attributed to the agency. However, if the foster parent is an "independent contractor," then the agency might not be liable for the negligent acts of the foster parent. One problem is that the foster parent-agency relationship has aspects of both independent contractor status and employee status. Employee or independent contractor status may also affect whether or not the foster parent is covered by the agency's insurance. Foster parents sometimes claim employee status because it enables them in certain instances to take advantage of insurance or immunity available only to employees. Public and private agencies, on the other hand, want the foster parents to be independent contractors so they can argue that they are not liable for their negligence.[43]

A very interesting case is *Vonner v. State through Dep't of Public Welfare*, 273 So. 2d 252 (La. 1973). *Vonner* is unusual because the court decided that in a situation involving intentional physical abuse inflicted by a foster parent to a foster child that resulted in death, the state "cannot delegate its legal responsibility ... to others" and is liable for injuries in a wrongful death suit. Subsequently, in another Louisiana case, *Cathey v. Bernard*, 467 So.2d 9 (La. Ct.App 1985), it was decided that *Vonner* does not mean that the "state is absolutely liable for all harm to a foster child, nor does [Vonner] make the state an insurer of the child's safety." Nonetheless, the court decided that *Vonner* made the "state liable for harm to a foster child that results from the tortious conduct of the foster parents." In other words, if the foster parents were negligent the state could also be found to be liable for the damages. The foster parents in *Cathey* were found to have been negligent for leaving a loaded gun on a closet shelf. This behavior was not an exercise of the "extraordinary" care called for by foster parents. More recently, in *Miller v. Martin* 838 So.2d 761 (La. 2003), the state argued that because of a change in the law the state could not be held liable for the intentional torts of foster parents. The *Miller* case is informative in so far as it contrasts the differing views of liability for state agencies. *Miller* upheld *Vonner* ruling that "if the foster parents fail in their own duty and abuse the children, the [state] is vicariously liable for those acts of the foster parents ..." Both the majority and the dissent in *Miller* noted that the decision is contrary to the laws of other states.

It is very difficult for some people to accept that even in situations where children are intentionally and seriously harmed in a foster home, the agency is not liable. However, liability is founded on fault and fault rests on negligence. Assume that while mowing the lawn a foster parent accidentally injures a foster child. Why should the agency be liable for the injury? Even if the foster parent was negligent the agency would not be found to have been negligent. Without negligence (or fault), agencies are not liable unless, as the *Vonner* case illustrates, state law made the agency vicariously liable for the negligence of the foster parents. Vicarious liability in the context of foster care can be thought of as a prohibition on the agency's ability to avoid responsibility for the actions of the foster parents. In other words, the agency cannot delegate its responsibility for care and safety of children to the effect that it is not liable for injuries to the child caused by the negligence of the foster parents.

C. When are Foster Care Agencies Immune from Suit?

Immunity means that one cannot be sued at all or even if sued cannot be held liable for the damages inflicted. Immunity is an important but somewhat difficult concept to grasp. A full discussion of immunity and its legal and policy implications are beyond the scope of this book.

There are different kinds of immunity.[44] Historically, governments were protected from suit by " sovereign immunity" and could not be sued at all. Many states have eliminated sovereign immunity, usually by enacting legislation but sometimes by judicial decision, so that government agencies and employees can be sued. Some states have eliminated immunity but enacted laws that only allow certain kinds of lawsuits. Sometimes suits are permitted only if certain conditions are met, such as prior notification of an intent to sue or proof that a specific statue has been violated. For example, *M.D.R. v. State ex rel. Human Services Dep't*, 836 P.2d 106, (N.M.App.1992), reveals that New Mexico eliminated immunity for certain state activities but not for foster care. To make the issue of immunity even more confusing, sometimes immunity in a specific situation can be based on the kind of decision making involved. Sometimes governmental immunity prevents individual employees, such as social workers and caseworkers, from being sued if they are engaged in a discretionary act, that is, an act requiring the exercise of judgment. *Kara B. by Albert v. Dane County*, 542 N.W.2d 777 (Wis. Ct. App. 1995)(Discretionary act immunity granted for claims brought by sexually abused foster child based on the principle that the agency's actions were discretionary).

D. Agency's Duty to Disclose Information to Foster Parents

From time to time, foster children injure foster parents or the biological child of the foster parent. In such circumstances, agencies can be liable based on their failure to warn of dangers or their negligence in even making the placement. In *P.G. v. State Dep't of Health and Human Services Div of Family & Youth Services*, 4 P.3d 326 (Ak. 2000), the foster parents sued the state after the foster child physically and sexually assaulted their two biological children. The foster parents alleged that the state had failed to disclose information that would have alerted them to the risks presented by the foster child. The court ruled that there was a duty to disclose such information and that a jury could find that the foster child's actions were a foreseeable result of the breach of the duty to disclose. In this case the foster care agency had presented the 13-year-old boy to the foster parents as "a really good kid" who "had never been in any trouble before" and "had no problems." This information was false. The boy "Billy" had been in trouble and had serious emotional, mental, and behavioral problems. The court concluded that the state has a duty to gather and present accurate information.

Another example is *Talle v. Nebraska Department of Social Services,*249 Neb 20, 541 N.W.2d 30 (1995), which addressed the liability of the placing agency when a foster child injured biological children in the foster home. (A subsequent case, *Talle v. Nebraska* [Talle II], 572 N.W.2d 790, (Neb. 1998) addressed only damages.) In *Talle* a foster parent sued the state claiming that she had been injured by a 13-year-old foster child placed into her home. The foster parents were not told that the child had a history of suicidal and homicidal threats and self-mutilation behaviors including physical abuse. The *Talle* parents took him as a foster child in accordance with an agreement stating that the agency would "share [with the foster parents] prior to placement and during placement, information known about the child's life situation as appropriate and necessary, …." Talle claimed that they never got information about "violent behavior" or "professional observations and opinions" regarding violent behavior. The physical and verbal assaults occurred over several months. There were no demands by Talle to remove the child and the foster family obtained guardianship over the child as recommended by the agency. The agency claimed that the foster family had "assumed the risk" of the injuries that had occurred, that is, the foster parents knew that being foster parents could expose them to getting hurt yet voluntarily became the foster parents of this particular foster child with the knowledge they could get injured. The court ruled that Talle did not "assume the risk," because she did not know of or understand the danger. The agency lied to Talle and encouraged her to continue her care of the foster child by telling her that the troubling behaviors were "a stage". The agency "actively prevented [the foster parent] from fully understanding the danger she was experiencing". Talle prevailed and was awarded damages.[45]

The duty to disclose usually rests on a statute that requires information to be provided. Sometimes, however, the "duty to disclose" is not a mandatory duty imposed on the agency such as when the "duty" is contained in a statute about foster parents' rights. In any event, duty to disclose situations usually turn on the details. Rarely are foster parents told everything about the children placed into their care. It would also seem that the cases finding a duty to disclose involve facts that are clearly the sort that should be disclosed.

E. Liability of the Agency for Foster Children who Injure Other Foster Children

Cases in which foster children injure other children are rare. One of the few cases to discuss this issue is *Reed v. Knox County Department of Human Services*, 968 F. Supp 1212 (D.S.D. Ohio 1997). Two foster children injured the foster parents' biological children and the foster parents sued the agency for the injuries. One of the arguments made by the foster parents, rejected by the court, was that the state was responsible for the injuries because the state acted *in loco parentis* and that therefore the state was for the actions of its wards, the foster children.[46] The court also said that state-arranged foster care "was not a one-sided undertaking forced on the foster parents by the state since the placement also required the agreement of the foster parents. Under this agreement, [the foster parents] assumed some degree of responsibility for the supervision of the foster children." In a 1997 case from Louisiana, *Edwards v. Burgess*, 700 So.2d 1129 (La. Ct.App. 1997), a foster child hit another child (not the foster parents' child) with a dart. The injured child's parents sued both the state and the foster parents of the child throwing the dart. Louisiana law provides that the "father and the mother [and tutors]...are responsible for the damage occasioned by their minor or unemancipated children ...". La. Civil Code Article 2318. The court concluded that the term "their minor or unemancipated children" did not apply to foster children and, therefore, neither the foster parents nor the state were liable for the foster child's actions. The court also concluded that neither the state nor the foster parents were negligent because it was not proven that either the foster parents or the state had failed to supervise the foster child.[47]

F. Insurance for Liability

It was at one time quite common for government agencies to purchase commercial insurance policies to insure against certain kinds of losses. Now, for a variety of reasons such insurance is either no longer available, is prohibitively expensive or even if it is available, its coverage is limited. Therefore, government agencies are usually "self insured." Claims for damages and the costs of lawsuits are paid from general revenue. Some jurisdictions budget money to pay for possible losses from and to defend against lawsuits. Most agencies have "risk-management offices" that assess the agencies exposure to liability, take steps to minimize such risks, and establish protocols to guide the agency's response when liability occurs.

G. Class Action Lawsuits

Sometimes public foster care agencies get sued because the entire foster care system has allegedly failed to care for children in accordance with applicable laws. These law suits, called class action suits, are designed to force agencies to improve foster care, for example, by cutting down on the length of time children spend in foster care.[48] An examination of such suits is found in Susan Gluck Mezey, PITIFUL PLAINTIFFS: CHILD WELFARE LITIGATION AND FEDERAL COURTS, (2000). These lawsuits have serious consequences for public foster care agencies. Initially, the agency involved must make a decision between contesting the lawsuit or agreeing to work out a settlement with the plaintiff's lawyers. A settlement is usually a detailed plan requiring the agency to make significant changes in the operation of the foster care system. Sometimes the agreement requires the dismissal or suspension of the lawsuit. A class action can also result in a court order that is enforced by the judge. These court orders can require structural or programmatic changes and impose performance criteria on the agency, such as the length of time it takes to respond to a reported allegation of child abuse. In some situations control of the child welfare system is taken away from the government and actually placed into the hands of the court or a court appointed receiver. This happened in Washington D.C. as a result of the LaShawn A. lawsuit. *LaShawn A. v. Dixon*, 762 F.Supp. 959 (D.D.C. 1991)(Finding a constitutional liberty interest in appropriate placement and case planning to prevent harm to children in District's custody), aff'd and remanded on other grounds sub.nom. *LaShawn A. by Moore v. Kelly*, 301 U.S.App.D.C. 49, 990 F.2d 1319 (D.C. Cir 1993).

Class actions also affect the degree of control the public agency will have over the delivery of foster care services. It should be noted that the number and outcome of these lawsuits is taken by many to signify a failure of foster care and has spurred discussion about other ways foster care can be organized. See, Mark E. Courtney and Maluccio, Anthony N. *The Rationalization of Foster Care in the Twenty-First Century* in Patrick A. Curtis, *et al.* eds. THE FOSTER CARE CRISIS: TRANSLATING RESEARCH into POLICY and PRACTICE (CHILD, YOUTH AND FAMILY SERVICES), (U. Nebraska Press 1999.)

H. Conclusion

Liability is not an issue that will disappear any time soon. Therefore, agencies need to constantly reevaluate their risk-management programs and ensure that all aspects of their foster care programs adhere to best practices. When evaluating specific instances of potential liability the most important questions include:

- Was the agency responsible for the welfare of the individual injured?
- Is the agency responsible for the specific actions of the individual that caused the injury?
- If the foster parent injured a foster child did the agency properly certify, train, and monitor the foster parent?
- Did the agency properly monitor the care of the child in the foster home?
- Did the agency react properly to indications of problems or unusual situations?
- Is the agency immune from suit or if not, does it have any defenses to liability?

IV. Liability Under Federal Civil Rights Law

A. Overview

A personal injury lawsuit (also called a tort case), is brought in state court. In addition to these personal injury cases there are also lawsuits based on violations of the civil rights of the injured individual. Foster children have used the federal civil rights law when suing public foster care agencies. These suits are brought under 42 U.S.C. §1983 and are referred to as "1983 actions."

B. Agency Liability Under §1983.

Section 1983 protects people from government ("state") action that infringes upon their constitutional and federal statutory rights. When bringing a §1983 action, a foster child would have to prove that an individual acting under "color of state law" violated one of his or her constitutional or other federal rights. The Supreme Court has ruled that individuals in state custody have certain substantive due process rights under the Fourteenth Amendment. The Fourteenth Amendment ensures that states cannot take away a citizen's life, liberty, or property without due process of law. Foster children have also argued that they can sue under §1983 if the state has deprived them of rights created by such federal laws as the *Adoption Assistance and Child Welfare Act,*and other federal laws that can pertain to children, such as the *Americans with Disabilities Act*. In foster care situations, the "state action" requirement is met because it is now well accepted that a state has a legal obligation to the foster child which in turn is based on its special relationship with the child. When a state agency removes a child from the biological family and places the child under state supervision in a foster home, the state creates a relationship with the child that invokes §1983.[49] Therefore, in spite of the ruling in the Deshaney case, foster children are owed a duty of care by the state agency.

C. The Professional Judgment and Deliberate Indifference Standards.

Just because a foster child has been injured under conditions that entitle the filing of a §1983 lawsuit does not mean that anyone will be found to have been liable. It must still be proven that a right protected by §1983 has been violated. It needs to be emphasized that §1983 is not violated merely because a foster child has been injured, even if the injury was negligently or even intentionally caused. Rather, a §1983 violation occurs when the negligent conduct is more than just negligence. As stated in *K.H. ex rel. Murphy v. Morgan*, 914 F.2d 846 (7th Cir. 1990), "[M]erely negligent…misconduct by state officers is not actionable under Section 1983." In other words, §1983 applies to situations that can be characterized by actions that exceed gross negligence.[50] The inability to sue under §1983 does not mean that the injured child cannot sue at all. It means that a suit would have to brought under state law if at all. (*Wells v. State*, 642 A.2d 879, (Md. App. 1994)(Violation of state mandated procedures may allow an action under state law but does not constitute a violation of due process of law).

Whenever a liability determination must be made, the most important legal issue is what standard is being used to assess the behavior of the agency or individual accused of negligence. In §1983 lawsuits, there are two standards that are being applied by the courts. One is known as the deliberate indifference standard and the other is the professional judgement standard.[51] *T.M. v. Carson*, 93 F. Supp 2d 1179 (D.Wy 2000), is noteworthy because, in discussing the professional judgement and deliberate indifference standards, the court remarked that "[a]s applied to a foster care setting we doubt that there is much difference in the two standards".[52]

The application of any standard to actual situations, whether deliberate indifference, professional judgment or something else, can be quite difficult. However, it is clear that adhering to professional standards and laws and regulations will always be a safe haven from accusations of deliberate indifference or failure of professional judgement.[53] For example, in the *T.M.* case the foster parents' file was missing and there was a dispute over the procedure used to place the subsequently abused children into the foster home, including allegations that the social worker and supervisor failed to properly conduct a home study, did not interview or train the foster parents, did not obtain references, and did not conduct a background investigation. Expert witnesses testified in essence that no social worker who had exercised professional judgment would have placed children into the home. In *Braam ex rel. Braam v. State of Washington*, 81 P.3d 851 (Wash. 2003) the Supreme Court of Washington helpfully compares the deliberate indifferent and professional judgment standard and offers a compelling explanation of why the professional judgment standard is most appropriate in foster care situations. Another recent case of interest is *Weatherford ex. Rel. Michael L. v. State*, 81 P.3d 320 (Az. 2003) (Sexual assault of a twelve-year old while at a group foster care facility).[54]

D. Immunity

In lawsuits against individual social workers under the federal civil rights law, "qualified immunity" may be available. Qualified immunity protects government employees from suit so long as their conduct does not violate clearly established statutory or constitutional rights "of which a reasonable person would have known."[55]

E. Foster Parents as State Actors Under Federal Civil Rights Law

Another issue of importance although one rarely ruled upon is whether or not foster parents can be state actors and thus subject to suit under §1983. Usually the answer is no, but on occasion the facts of a particular case may cause the court to rule otherwise.[56] For example, in *Howard v. Malac*, 270 F. Supp. 2d 132 (D. Mass. 2003), it was alleged that a foster mother abused a foster child and that she "colluded with" state social workers to "cover it up." The court did conclude that usually, foster parents are not state agents for §1983 purposes, but also explained that there are certain situations in which the foster parent/private actor can be so closely "entwined" in the state's conduct that the private actor can be a state actor under §1983.

F. Section 1983 Liability and Private Foster Care Agencies

Can a private foster care agency be found to have violated §1983? There is no consistent response to this question. Because §1983 was intended to encompass abuse of state authority, most lawsuits involving foster care are brought against state agencies. However, private agencies and employees or private agencies are sued under §1983. However, there are very few cases addressing the circumstances that will determine whether a private foster care agency or its employees will be liable under §1983. The opinions differ in their reasoning and conclusions. For example, in *Doe v. New York City Department of Social Services,* 649 F.2d 134 (2d Cir 1981), a leading case regarding foster care agency liability under §1983, it seems to have been assumed that §1983 applied to a private foster care agency. In a case involving the obligation of a private agency to search for and find the biological father of a child in foster care, it was assumed without analysis that the private agency was susceptible to §1983 liability. *Daniel H. v. City of New York et al,* 115 F.Supp 2d 423 (S.D.N.Y. 2000). There are cases that have concluded that neither private agencies or their employees are "state actors" for §1983 purposes.[57]

G. Conclusion

If a public foster care agency is sued for injuries to a foster child, it is likely that at least part of lawsuit will be based on §1983 claims. Therefore, all agencies need to be familiar with previous lawsuits in their jurisdiction and need to stay aware of new decisions in this area. In addition, agencies should especially be alert to cases that address immunity and foster parent liability under §1983 since such changes could broaden or constrict exposure to liability. Whenever it appears that an agency has been or is likely to be sued under §1983, the agency should quickly begin to address the following:

- Whether the agency or its employees have violated any federal or state statues or regulations
- Whether the agency or any of its employees have acted negligently
- If it appears that a foster child's constitutional rights have been violated, the agency needs to determine the "standard of care" that will be applied and whether the agency is at risk of being found to have breached that standard of care.
- If negligent or potentially negligent behavior is detected the agency will need to determine if the negligent behavior will trigger §1983 liability.
- If liability appears likely, the agency needs to determine if there are any immunity issues.
- If foster parents may be negligent, it must be determined whether there a possibility that the foster parents are susceptible to §1983 liability.

V. Private Agency Liability

A. Overview

Under what circumstances will the private agency be financially responsible when someone is killed or injured? When a foster child, foster parent, or someone else is injured the private agency can be sued and, if found to have acted negligently, can be required to pay financial compensation to the injured party. Almost always the lawsuits are brought by or on behalf of foster children or their estates, alleging that they were injured (or killed) by their foster parents. There are also cases that involve injuries to a foster parent by foster children and cases that involve injuries to property or persons by foster children.

Any attempt to ascertain the liability of an agency for a particular event must start with the laws and judicial opinions of the state in which the event occurred or in some instances where the agency operates or where the suit was filed. Because laws and judicial decisions differ from state to state, so do the contours of private agency liability. Nonetheless, there are common issues that are generally applicable to all private foster care agencies in all states.

Private foster care agencies can be sued whenever a child is injured in foster care or the child injures another person. Like other entities, the agency itself can be sued or the individual social workers or other employees can be sued. The traditional basis for a lawsuit against a private agency (as with a public agency) would be negligence. That is, did the agency or one of its employees act or refrain from acting in such a way as to cause the injury? For example, using the most frequent situation, if the foster child is injured by a foster parent, the relevant issue would be whether or not the agency failed to insure the safety of the foster child in the foster home. The essential elements would be the evaluation of the foster parents, the correctness of placing the child into that particular home, and whether the agency properly monitored the placement and reacted properly to suspicions of substandard care or other events that reasonably should cause the agency to question the adequacy of the placement. When an agency is accused of liability, it usually is based on the allegation that the agency knew or should have known about risk to the child if placed into, or remaining in, that foster home.

B. Immunity from Suit

As previously discussed, some jurisdictions provide immunity from suit for public agencies. If a private agency is providing foster care under contract to a public agency and is therefore doing just what the public agency does, it too may be immune from suit in those situations in which the public agency would be immune. Sometimes a statute will create immunity for certain kinds of activities pertaining to the protection of children and such law will apply equally to public and private agencies. *Lara v. City of New York,* 187 Misc. 2d 882, 726 N.Y.S.2d 217 (N.Y. Sup. 2001) (Providing services to children). Usually the answer is not so definite and the issue becomes whether the private agency providing care under contract can share in the immunity that protects the government.[58]

C. Delegation of Authority to Care for Children

Another issue that arises in liability cases is the relationship between the private agency and the public agency. When an injured party sues a private agency, it usually also sues all other entities that might have been negligent. When the private agency is sued the public agency gets sued as well. An issue seldom addressed in the courts is how a delegation of authority from public to private agency relates to liability of the private agency. Can responsibility for the proper care of foster children be delegated in such a manner as to prevent liability from attaching to the public agency? In other words, if the private agency acts negligently, is the public agency either strictly or vicariously liable for this negligence? Thus far the answer seems to be no. For example, in one of the few cases to address public-private negligence in the context of the state's authority to delegate, the court decided that the state was allowed to delegate care for foster children and that the public agency could not be held liable for the negligence of the private agency.[59]

D. Private Agency Claim to the Protections of Parental Immunity

A new issue has arisen that bears close attention: whether or not the protections of parental immunity can be claimed by a private agency. As seen in Chapter Two on foster parents, there are jurisdictions that allow foster parents to claim immunity from suit just as biological parents can claim such immunity. That being so, can it be argued that foster parents are agents or employees of the private agency acting in the place of the biological parents? If so, ought the private agency be immune from suit whenever a biological parent would be immune? The answer so far has been no. In what might be the only case to deal with this precise issue, it was determined that parental immunity would not be extended to a private agency providing residential care to a child. *Wallace v. Smyth, et al.,* 762 N.E.2d 83, 327 Ill. App. 3d 411

(App.Ct.Ill) rev'd and remanded, *Wallace v. Smyth et al*, 786 N.E.2d 980, (Ill. 2002); cert. denied by *Maryville Academy v. Wallace*, 124 S.Ct. 43 (2003).

E. Insurance

Foster care agencies, like all responsible organizations that care for children, are covered by insurance policies. Usually, such policies are required by the state agency that contracts with the private agency. Policies vary greatly in coverage, exclusions, and other matters. For foster parent insurance, and issues related to injuries to foster parents by foster children, see Chapter Two on foster parents.

F. Conclusion

As ought to be evident, private foster care agencies get sued with enough frequency to impose upon them the same "risk-management" paradigm as public agencies. Among the most critical issues for a private agency are:

- What is the relationship between the private agency and the public agency as it relates to liability and indemnification?
- Does the agency have the right kind of and enough insurance?
- Are all agency staff well versed in when and how to respond to incidents and situations that might give rise to liability?
- What is the legal relationship of the agency to its foster parents and how does this relationship affect liability?
- What is the current state of the law in the agency's jurisdiction regarding liability and related matters?

VI. Summary—Essential Elements of Liability for Injury to Foster Child

In terms of foster care, the most usual liability situation involves injuries to a foster child inflicted by a foster parent or resulting from a foster parent's negligence. Usually the foster children bring a lawsuit against the agency and the social workers responsible for the foster home. In this situation, there are some common issues that almost always present. Assume that in a public agency foster home it is discovered that the foster father has been molesting the foster child. Assessing liability calls for a number of questions to be asked:

- Can the foster father himself be sued or is he for some reason immune from being sued?
- If there is a foster mother is she negligent for not knowing about or preventing the molestation?
- Even if either or both foster parents can be sued do they have financial resources to pay damages?
- Do the foster parents have insurance that would cover any damages?
- Is the agency liable under state law for the injuries?
- Is the agency immune from suit (under state law)?
- Is the agency or its employees liable under §1983?
- If §1983 is relevant can any of the social workers claim immunity?
- If there is §1983 liability what standard will be used to determine liability?
- Is the agency liable for the actions of the foster parents?
- Are the foster parents agents or employees of the agency or are they independent contractors? How does this affect liability?
- Can the foster parents be sued under §1983?
- Could the agency or any social worker of the agency have acted differently and would this have prevented the injury?
- Were the foster parents properly evaluated, certified, and trained?
- Did the agency properly monitor the child's care and investigate any signs that anything was amiss?
- Did the social worker visit the child in the home or at school?
- Did the worker interview and talk to the child and react promptly to complaints or indications of problems?
- Did the agency's role in any way fall below the duty the agency owed to the child?
- Were any specific statutes, regulations, policies, or procedures violated?
- Are there any insurance or indemnification issues relevant to the agency?

If the agency was a private and not a public foster care agency, there are additional considerations:

- Is the public agency liable if it did not properly monitor the private agency?
- Can the public agency delegate its responsibility to care for foster children to the private agency?
- Is the private agency subject to a §1983 suit?
- Is there any basis for finding that that private agency is not liable for the actions of the foster parents or is immune from suit?

APPENDIX B

FLOW CHART
How Children Enter and Leave Foster Care

Report and investigation of suspected child maltreatment

Child is removed and placed into foster care
OR
Parents request agency's services and child is placed in foster care

Investigation case is closed and child returned home
(sometimes with services to family)
OR
Case is petitioned into court AND
Child is returned home under agency monitoring
OR
Child remains in foster care pending judicial process AND
Reunification services begin or are deemed inappropriate
(Child could be returned home before trial under agency supervision)

At trial the allegations of maltreatment are proven
OR
The parent agrees that maltreatment occurred AND
Child is returned home under agency supervision
OR
Child remains in foster care AND
Reunification services proceed or are deemed not appropriate AND
Case is reviewed periodically AND
Child is eventually returned home
OR
Parental rights are relinquished or terminated and
child is eventually adopted
OR

Child is permanently placed with relatives, a legal guardian,
or in independent living
OR
A "compelling reason" is found for another placement

APPENDIX C

How to Find a Legal Case

If you wish to read a court case, an easy free way to find cases is through www.findlaw.com. Both federal and state statutes and regulations can be found at http://Thomas.loc.gov. Here is how to find a case:

Most foster care cases are heard in a state trial court. Most state trial court cases are not published. If the case is appealed, however, and the issues are important, the opinion of the court of appeals and of the state's highest court may be published. Published state court cases can usually be found in two places: a state reporter and and a regional reporter. There are seven regional reporters: Northeast (N.E.) Atlantic (A.), Southeast (S.E.), Southern (So.), Southwest (S.W.), Northwest (N.W.) and Pacific (P.). Most of the cases referred to in *Foster Care Law: A Primer* cite only to the regional reporters that can be found in every law school library and also on-line. A typical citation is:

In re Weiler, 581 S.E.2d 134 (N.C. 2003)

The case name is *In re Weiler.*. It is found in volume 581 of the second series of the Southeast Reporter at page 134. It is a North Carolina case that was decided in 2003.

California is an exception to the regional reporters: since 1959 it has published cases in its state reporters. California cases in *Foster Care Law: A Primer* will be cited like this:

In re Luke L., 52 Cal Rptr.2d 53 (Cal.Ct.App.1996)

New York, also an exception, publishes many cases that are not found in the Northeastern Reporter, some from lower courts. For example:

Andrews v. Otsego County, 446 N.Y.S. 2d 169 (Sup.Ct. 1982)

The system for decoding California and New York cases is the same as for regional reporters.

Certain kinds of foster care cases can be brought in federal court, for example class actions, and appeals of special education findings. If they are important cases from the federal court of appeals they will appear in the Federal Reporter. A typical citation is:

Jensen v. Lane County, 222 F.3d 570 (9th Cir. 2000)

If it is an important case heard in the trial court (the District court) it may appear in the Federal Supplement reporter, like this:

Donlan v. Ridge, 58 F. Supp. 2d 604 (E.D. Pa. 1999)

One reads this as volume 58 of the second series of the Federal Supplement, page 604, a case decided in the Eastern District of Pennsylvania in 1999.

Cases from both state and federal courts ultimately may be resolved by the U.S. Supreme Court. There are three reporters for cases from the highest court. In *Foster Care Law: A Primer* we cite only to the United States Reports. Citations appear as:

Bellotti v. Baird, 443 U.S. 622 (1979)

Cases that have not yet been published, or perhaps are not scheduled to be published but are considered by lawyers to be important nevertheless, are found in the professional on-line data bases managed by Westlaw and Lexis. Cases from those systems are cited with the initials WL, or LEXIS, as in:

Weatherford v. Arizona, Supreme Court of Arizona,
Dec. 12, 2003, 2003 Ariz. LEXIS 143

Citations to law review articles follow the same patterns as cases:

Bernadette W. Hartfield, *The Role of the Interstate Compact
on the Placement of Children in Interstate Adoption,*
68 Neb.L.Rev. 292 (1982)

The article on interstate adoption is found in volume 68 of the Nebraska Law Review at page 292. It was published in 1982.

Appendix D

Selected Provisions of the Adoption and Safe Families Act of 1997

P.L. 105-89, 42 U.S.C. §§620–679

Date Foster Care Commences

42 U.S.C. §675(5)
(§475(5) of the Act)

(F) a child shall be considered to have entered foster care on the earlier of—
    (i) the date of the first judicial finding that the child has been subjected to child abuse or neglect; or
    (ii) the date that is 60 days after the date on which the child is removed from the home.

Reasonable efforts

42 U.S.C. §671 (a)
(§471 of the Act)

In order for a State to be eligible for payments under this part, it shall have a plan approved by the Secretary which—

(15) provides that—
    (A) in determining reasonable efforts to be made with respect to a child, as described in this paragraph, and in making such reasonable efforts, the child's health and safety shall be the paramount concern;
    (B) except as provided in subparagraph (D), reasonable efforts shall be made to preserve and reunify families—

       (i) prior to the placement of a child in foster care to prevent or eliminate the need for removing the child from the child's home; and

      (ii) to make it possible for a child to safely return to the child's home.

(C) if continuation of reasonable efforts of the type described in subparagraph (B) is determined to be inconsistent with the permanency plan for the child, reasonable efforts shall be made to place the child in a timely manner in accordance with the permanency plan, and to complete whatever steps are necessary to finalize the permanent placement of the child;

(D) reasonable efforts of the type described in subparagraph (B) shall not be required to be made with respect to a parent of a child if a court of competent jurisdiction has determined that

    (i) the parent has subjected the child to aggravated circumstances (as defined in State law, which definition may include but need not be limited to abandonment, torture, chronic abuse and sexual abuse);

    (ii) the parent has

       (I) committed murder (which would have been an offense under section 1111(a) of title 18, United States Code, if the offense had occurred in the special maritime or territorial jurisdiction of the United States) of another child of the parent;

      (II) committed voluntary manslaughter (which would have been an offense under section 1112(a) of title 18, United States Code, if the offense had occurred in the special maritime or territorial jurisdiction of the United States) of another child of the parent;

     (III) aided or abetted, attempted, conspired, or solicited to commit such a murder or such a voluntary manslaughter; or

     (IV) committed a felony assault that results in serious bodily injury to the child or another child of the parent; or

    (iii) the parental rights of the parent to a sibling have been terminated involuntarily;

(E) if reasonable efforts of the type described in subparagraph (B) are not made with respect to a child as a result of a determination made by a court of competent jurisdiction in accordance with subparagraph (D)—

(i) a permanency hearing (as described in section 475(5)(c) shall be held for the child within 30 days after the determination; and

(ii) reasonable efforts shall be made to place the child in a timely manner in accordance with the permanency plan and to complete whatever steps are necessary to finalize the permanent placement of the child; and

(F) reasonable efforts to place a child for adoption or with a legal guardian may be made concurrently with reasonable efforts of the type described in subparagraph (B);

Reunification Services

42 U.S.C. §629a (a)
(§431 of the Act)

(7) Time—Limited Family Reunification Services—

(A) In General-The term 'time-limited family reunification services' means the services and activities described in subparagraph (B) that are provided to a child that is removed from the child's home and placed in a foster family home or a child care institution and to the parents or primary caregiver of such a child, in order facilitate the reunification of the child safely and appropriately within a timely fashion, but only during the 15-month period that begins on the date that the child, pursuant to section 475(5)(F), is considered to have entered foster care.

(B) Services and Activities Described.—The services and activities described in this subparagraph are the following:

(i) Individual, group and family counseling.

(ii) Inpatient, residential, or outpatient substance abuse treatment services.

(iii) Mental health services.

(iv) Assistance to address domestic violence.

(v) Services designed to provide temporary child care and therapeutic services for families, including crisis nurseries.

(vi) Transportation to or from any of the services and activities described in this subparagraph.

Foster parents' notice of hearings

42 U.S.C. §675(5)
(§475(5) of the Act)

(G) the foster parents (if any) of a child and any preadoptive parent or relative providing care for the child are provided with notice of, and an opportunity to be heard in, any review or hearing to be held with respect to the child, except that this subparagraph shall not be construed to require that any foster parent, preadoptive parent, or relative providing care for the child be made a party to such a review or hearing solely on the basis of such notice and opportunity to be heard.

Case review system; permanency hearings

42 U.S.C. §675
(§ 475 of the Act)

(5) The term "case review system" means a procedure for assuring that—
.…
(B) the status of each child is reviewed periodically but no less frequently than once every six months by a court or by administrative review (as defined in paragraph (6)) in order to determine the safety of the child, the continuing necessity for and appropriateness of the placement, the extent of compliance with the case plan, and the extent of progress which has been made toward alleviating or mitigating the causes necessitating placement in foster care, and to project a likely date by which the child may be returned to and safely maintained in the home or placed for adoption or legal guardianship,
(C) with respect to each such child, procedural safeguards will be applied, among other things, to assure each child in foster care under the supervision of the State of a permanency hearings to be held, in a family or juvenile court or another court (including a tribal court) of competent jurisdiction, or by an administrative body appointed or approved by the court, no later than 12 months after the date the child is considered to have entered foster care (as determined under subparagraph (F) (and not less frequently than every 12 months thereafter during the continuation of foster care), which hearing shall determine the permanency plan for the child that includes whether, and if applicable when, the child will be returned to the parent, placed for adoption and the State will file a petition for termination of parental rights, or referred for legal guardianship, or (in cases where the State agency has documented to the State court a compelling reason for determining that it

would not be in the best interests of the child to return home, be referred for termination of parental rights, or be placed for adoption, with a fit and willing relative, or with a legal guardian) placed in another planned permanent living arrangement and, in the case of a child described in subparagraph (A)(ii), whether the out-of-State placement continues to be appropriate and in the best interests of the child, and, in the case of a child who has attained age 16, the services needed to assist the child to make the transition from foster care to independent living; and procedural safeguards shall also be applied with respect to parental rights pertaining to the removal of the child from the home of his parents, to a change in the child's placement, and to any determination affecting visitation privileges of parents.

Appendix E

Selected Bibliography and Resources

Books and Journals

American Bar Association, Making Sense of ASFA Regulations: a roadmap for effective implementation. American Bar Association: Wash. D.C. (2001)
   A thorough legal analysis of regulations interpreting ASFA, including the text of the regulations.

American Bar Association. *Standards of Practice for Lawyers Representing a Child in Abuse and Neglect Cases.* http://www.abanet.org/child
   Practice standards include ethics in representing clients with "diminished capacity."

Association of Administrators of the Interstate Compact on the Placement of Children, Compact Administrators' manual, American Public Human Services Association, Wash. D.C. (updated continually)
   Explains processes to follow in placing a child under the ICPC. Very helpful.

Bennett, Paul, Symposium, *Hearing Children's Voices: Secret Reflections: Some Thoughts About Secrets and Court Processes in Child Protection Matters,* 45 Ariz. L.Rev. 713 (2003).
   An interesting discussion of a subject rarely dealt with—children and privacy in child welfare matters.

Cavenaugh, Karen and Daniel Pollack. *Liability Protections for Foster Parents.* 6 Kan. J.L.Pub.Pol. 78 (Sum/Fall 1997).
   Argues that foster parents should be given liability protection in order to encourage recruitment of foster parents, and cites theories under which state courts have decided liability cases and legislatures have addressed

them, including 1) in loco parentis, 2) indemnification, and 3) commercial insurance.

Child Welfare League of America, CHILD MALTREATMENT IN FOSTER CARE. CWLA BEST PRACTICE GUIDELINES. CWLA Press: Wash. D.C. (2003)

Child Welfare League of America, MAKING MANAGED HEALTH CARE WORK FOR KIDS IN FOSTER CARE, CWLA Press: Wash. D.C. (2000).
> Youth in foster care have so many health problems when they enter that they need even more intense screening and treatment than teens not in foster care. The League developed a Checklist of Needed Services for Children in Foster Care, including timelines for service.

Child Welfare League of America, STANDARDS OF EXCELLENCE FOR FAMILY FOSTER CARE SERVICES, Revised Edition, CWLA Press: Wash. D.C. (1995).
> Sets goals toward which public and private foster care agencies may aspire.

Child Welfare League of America, STANDARDS OF EXCELLENCE FOR SERVICES FOR ABUSED OR NEGLECTED CHILDREN AND THEIR FAMILIES, CWLA, Wash D.C.(1998).
> Replaces 1989 standards with goals that respond to changes in the law and account for evolving social service policy.

Courtney, Mark E. and Anthony N. Maluccio. *The Rationalization of Foster Care in the Twenty-First Century,* in Patrick A. Curtis, *et al,* eds. THE FOSTER CARE CRISIS, U. Nebraska Press (1999).
> Authors speculate very creatively about the future of foster care. Factors they consider are aging population, racism, fertility technology, work-based reform, information systems and managed care.

Cunningham, Thomas J., *Considering Religion as a Factor in Foster Care in the Aftermath of Employment Division, Dept. of Human Resources v. Smith and the Religious Freedom Restoration Act,* 28 U. Rich. L.Rev. 53 (1994).

Dale, Michael J., *et al,* Eds., REPRESENTING THE CHILD CLIENT, Lexis Publishing (2000)
> An excellent reference on juvenile law practice that includes one chapter on neglect-abuse practice, referencing to many child welfare resources.

Dogin, Janet L., *Just a Gene: Judicial Assumptions about Parenthood,* 40 UCLA L. Rev. 637 (Feb. 1993).
> Helps practitioner analyze when notice and opportunity to be heard on a custody issue must be extended to an unmarried father

Duggan, Maureen S., Annotation, *Failure of State or Local Government Entity to Protect Child Abuse Victim as Violation of Federal Constitutional Right,* 79 A.L.R. Fed. 514 (1986 Supp. 2002).

Edwards, Leonard. *Judicial Oversight of Parental Visitation in Family Reunification Cases,* 54 Juvenile and Family Court Journal 1, (Summer 2003).
    Describes and advocates for strong judicial intervention to arrange visitation. Explains evolution of California cases.

Elster, Arthur B., & Zuznets, Naomi J., *AMA Guidelines for Adolescent Preventive Services: Recommendations and Rationale (GAPS),*Williams & Wilkins: Baltimore MD (1994).
    A guide for physicians that sets standards for adolescent health care. Strong on issues like sexually transmitted diseases and special education.

English, Abigail, Madlyn Morreale and Amy Stinnet. *Adolescents in Public Health Insurance programs: Medicaid and CHIP,* Center for Adolescent Health & the Law: Chapel Hill, North Carolina (1999)
    Excellent detailed description of health services that can be obtained by children through Medicaid and CHIP, including barriers.

Freundlich, Madelyn & Sarah Gerstenzang, AN ASSESSMENT OF THE PRIVATIZATION OF CHILD WELFARE SERVICES CHALLENGES AND SUCCESSES. CWLA Press: Wash.D.C. (2003).
    A detailed and comprehensive critical analysis of privatization efforts in Iowa and elsewhere.

Green, M. (ed.), *Bright Futures: Guidelines for Health Supervision of Infants, Children and Adolescents.* Nat. Center for Education in Maternal & Child Health. (1994).
    A guide for parents and physicians that sets standards of preventive health care for children according to their ages and stages of development.

Hartfield, Bernadette W., *The Role of the Interstate Compact on the Placement of Children in Interstate Adoption,* 68 Neb. Law Rev. 292 (1989).
    Describes the problems that the ICPC is meant to resolve.

Helwige, Jean, *Winning for Children,* 39(2) Trial 58 (2002)
    Interview with Marcia Robinson Lowry of Children's Rights organization. Contains useful data on the class action suits undertaken. (6 systems under court supervision, litigation against 3 more, and 3 under investigation.

Kearse, Brendan P., *Abused Again: Competing Constitutional Standards for the State's Duty to Protect Foster Children,* 29 Columbia J. L. & Soc. Probs. 385 (1996).

Explores Section 1983 civil rights cases relating to liability of a foster care agency.

Kennedy, Michael P., Comment, *In the Best Interest of the Child: Religious and Racial Matching in Foster Care,* 3 Geo. Mason U. Civ. Rts. L.J. 299 (1993).
Discusses racial and religious legal issues that can affect foster care.

Kramer, Donald T., (ed.), LEGAL RIGHTS OF CHILDREN. 2d Ed., Shepherd's/McGraw Hill (1994).
A three volume treatise examining the rights of children in general as well as in civil criminal and child abuse and neglect proceedings.

Kubitschek, Carolyn A., *Social Work Malpractice for Failure to Protect Foster Children,* 41 Am.Jur.Trials 1. (1990 Supp. 2002)
Detailed explanation of the legal aspects of social worker negligence.

Kussman, Patricia C., *Right of Indigent Parent to Appointed Counsel in Proceeding for Involuntary Termination of Parental Rights,* 92 ALR 5th 379 (2000)
Gathers cases relevant to appointment of counsel to indigent biological parents who are facing termination of parental rights cases.

Lens, Vicki, *The Supreme Court, Federalism and Social Policy: the New Judicial Activism,* June 2001 Social Service Review, 319-336.
Article relates to U.S.Supreme Court position on suits by citizens to enforce states to implement Federal laws.

Malik, Neena W., Mary M. Crowson, Cindy S. Lederman and Joy D. Osofsky. *Evaluating Maltreated Infants, Toddlers and Preschoolers in Dependency Court.* 23(5) Infant Mental Health Journal 576 (2002).
Describes a protocol to screen, assess and treat mental health issues in infants entering dependency court. Shows how courts and social service systems can work together, but also how one system can take over tasks usually belonging to the other.

Mangold, Susan Vivian, *Protection, Privatization and Profit in the Foster Care System,* 60 Ohio State Law Journal 1295 (1999).
An excellent article on privatization of foster care, explaining the various ways it can occur and what the hazards and benefits are.

Melsch, Lisa, *et al., Implementation of Family-Centered Treatment Program for Substance-Abusing Women and their Children: Barriers and Resolutions,* 27(1) Journal of Psychoactive Drugs 73 (1995).
Among other elements, describes how residential treatment programs interact with foster care agencies.

Miller, Michelle, *Revisiting Poor Joshua: State-Created Danger Theory in the Foster Care Context,* 11 Hastings Women's Law Journal 243 (2000)
　　Explores liability issues comparing the status of children who are almost-in foster care, to those who are in custody of the agency.

Moye, Jim & Roberta Rinker, *It's a Hard Knock Life: Does the Adoption and Safe Families Act of 1997 Adequately Address Problems in the Child Welfare System?* 39 Harv.J. on Leg. 375 (2002).
　　Authors fault ASFA for failing to give funds to recruit and retain foster care workers, permitting cases to be decided by judges who have no expertise in this law, failing to interface with other Federal laws like TANF and Medicaid, failing to make timelines sensitive to the resources, and giving bonuses for adoption but not for reunification. Proposes amendments to correct problems.

Murray, Kasia O'Neill, *The Child Welfare Financing Structure,* Pew Foundation, http://pewfostercare.org/docs/index/php?DocId=9.
　　A brief but quite useful guide to the various sources of federal child welfare.

Nadile, Vincent S. Note, *Promoting the Integrity of Foster Family Relationships: Needed Statutory Protections for Foster Parents,* 62 Notre Dame L.Rev. 899 (2002).
　　Examination of court decisions and legal principles pertaining to the foster parent-foster child relationship.

National Council of Juvenile and Family Court Judges and the American Public Human Services Assocation, THE INTERSTATE COMPACT ON THE PLACEMENT OF CHILDREN: MANUAL AND INSTRUCTIONAL GUIDE FOR JUVENILE AND FAMILY COURT JUDGES. NCJFCJ: Reno NV (2001).
　　Helpful material on the ICPC.

O'Conner, M., FEDERAL TAX BENEFITS FOR FOSTER AND ADOPTIVE PARENTS AND KINSHIP CAREGIVERS 2002 TAX YEAR. Publication No. 503, *Child and Dependent Tax Credit.* Publication No. 972, *Child Tax Credit.* Casey Family Programs: Seattle (2002)
　　Very good explanation of federal tax issues and foster care.

Patton, William Wesley, *The Status of Siblings' Rights: A View into the New Millenium,* 51 DePaul L.Rev.1 (2001).
　　Analysis of legal issues pertaining to sibling's rights.

Pollack, Daniel, *Liability Insurance for Foster Parents and Agencies: The Role of Commercial Insurers,* 4 Journal of Law & Social Work 1, (May 1993).
　　Explains this specialized area of liability law.

Pollack, Daniel, SOCIAL WORK AND THE COURTS: A CASEBOOK. (Brunner-Routledge 2d. Ed. 2003).
A broad collection of cases focused on decisions that address social work issues.

Reamer, Frederick G., SOCIAL WORK MALPRACTICE AND LIABILITY SRATEGIES FOR PREVENTION. Columbia Univ. Press (1994).
A very useful explanation of malpractice and negligence in the social work context.

Roberts, Dorothy, SHATTERED BONDS: THE COLOR OF CHILD WELFARE. Basic Books: N.Y. (2002).
An examination of racial influences on child protection and foster care.

Rosenfeld, A.A. *et al. Foster Care: An Update.* 36(4) Journal of the American Academy of Child and Adolescent Psychiatry 448 (1997).
Summarizing 20 years of health surveys, authors found that foster children have three to seven times as many acute and chronic health conditions, developmental delays and emotional adjustment problems as other poor children.

Samuels, Elizabeth J, *The Art of Line Drawing: the Establishment Clause and Public Aid to Religiously Affiliated Child Care,* 69 Ind.L.J. 39 (1993).
Analysis of legal aspects of public funding to faith-based organizations.

Shields, Marjorie J., *Power of Court or Other Public Agency to Order Vaccination Over Parent's Religious Objection,* 94 ALR 5th 613 (2001; Supp. 2003)
Gathers and sorts relevant cases, offering insight into cases that connect child's need for medical care with parental religious objection.

Simms, M.D. *et al, Health Care Needs of Children in the Foster Care System.* 106(4) Journal of the Ambulatory Pediatric Association 909 (Oct. 2000).
Authors describe how public agencies have actually created barriers to health care for foster children.

Sklar, Elliott D. YOU DON'T ALWAYS GET WHAT YOU PAY FOR: THE ECONOMICS OF PRIVATIZATION, Cornell U. Press (2000).
An intensive analysis of contracting out and privatization, although not addressing foster care or child welfare.

Smyth, Todd R., Annotation, *Foster Parent's Right to Immunity from Foster Child's Negligence Claims.* 55 A.L.R. 4th 778 (1987 Supp. 2002)

Soehnel, Sonja A., Annotation, *Governmental Tort Liability for Social Services Agency's Negligence in Placement, or Supervision after Placement, of Children.* 90 A.L.R.3d 1214 (1979 Supp. 2002)

U.S. Health and Human Services, BLENDING PERSPECTIVES AND BUILDING COMMON GROUND, A Report to Congress on Substance Abuse and Child Protection. (1999).
> Report states that children from substance-abusing families spent longer periods of time in foster care and were less likely to have left foster care with a year than other children in care.

Williams, John C. *Power of Court or Other Public Agency to order Medical Treatment for Child Over Parental Objections not Based on Religious Grounds,* 97 ALR 3d 421 (1980; Supp.2003)
> Offers relevant cases where a child's health needs are opposed by parents on basis of religion.

Wilson, Katherine S., Comment., *Not Quite a Family: The Second Circuit Decides Against Recognizing Procedural Due Process Rights for a Pre-Adoptive Foster Family in* Rodriguez v. McLouglin, 67 Brooklyn L.Rev. 899 (2002)
> Intensive analysis of the Rodriguez case.

Yiu, Karen W., Note, *Foster Parents as State Actors in Section 1983 Actions: What Rayburn v. Hogue Missed,* 7 U.C. Davis Journal of Law & Policy, 117 (2003).
> Critical examination of federal decision ruling that foster parents are not state actors.

Zawisza, Christina A. *Child Welfare Managed Care in Florida: Will it be Innovation or Abdication?* 25 Nova Law Review 619 (2001)
> A look at the recent privatization of Florida's foster care system.

Selected Federal Laws that Affect Foster Care

The Adoption and Safe Families Act of 1997, P.L. 105-89, 42 U.S.C. 620-679
> The basic law for foster care, amending the Social Security act. Among other things, it describes responsibilities of public foster care agencies, biological parents, courts, and to some extent foster parents.

The Americans with Disabilities Act of 1990, P.L. 101-336, 42 U.S.C. 121-1 *et seq..*
> Describes process for funding children with special needs

The Child Abuse Prevention and Treatment Act, P.L. 100-294, 42 U.S.C. 51006a as amend. 2003.

Sets certain standards for states to meet (for example, for representation of children) if they wish to obtain funds.

Early and Periodic Screening, Diagnostic and Treatment Services, the Medicaid Act, 42 U.S.C. s.1396(a) (43); 1396(d)(a)(4)(B); 1396(d)(r)
All child recipients of Medicaid (most children in foster care) are entitled to the comprehensive screening, diagnosis and treatment.

The Foster Care Independence Act of 1999, P.L. 106-169, 42 U.S.C. 677 *et seq.*
Extends many foster care services to youth who would otherwise age out of the foster care system. States can offer housing, education, and even Medicaid.

The Indian Child Welfare Act of 1978, *P.L. 95-608, 25 U.S.C. 1901-1963.*
Describes the separate processes that must be followed for Native American children, to give them—and the tribe—an opportunity to be raised in the culture.

The Individuals with Disabilities Education Act of 1975 as amended 1997, P.L. 105-17, 20 U.S.C. 677 *et seq.*
Sets forth requirements for children with special needs to receive a free and appropriate education and many related services.

The Multi-Ethnic Placement Act, P.L. 103-382, Title V, Part E., 42 U.S.C. 1996b
Assures that no child shall be turned down for an adoptive placement solely because the adoptive parents are of another culture or reside in another state.

Five On-Line Research Sites that Connect to other Useful Sites.

The American Bar Association Center on Children and the Law. http://www.abanet.org/child/home2.html

The Children's Bureau, U.S. Health and Human Services. http://www.acf.hhs.gov/programs/cb/index.htm

The Library of Congress. http://Thomas.loc.gov

The National Foster Parent Association. www.nfpainc.org

Westlaw free legal research site. www.Findlaw.com

NOTES

1. Examples of class action suits are *G.L. v. Stangler*, 873 F. Supp. 252 (W.D. Mo. 1994); *L.J. v. Massinga*,838 F. 2d 118 (4th Cir. 1988); *LaShawn A. v. Dixon*, 762 F. Supp. 959 (D.D.C.1991); *Marisol v. Giuliani*, 929 F. Supp. 662 (S.D. N.Y. 1996); *Sanders v. Lewis*, Docket No. 2:92-0353 (S.D.W.Va. Filed Mar. 1, 1995), 1995 W.L. 228308.

2. Refugee children in the unaccompanied minors program generally are not eligible for adoption. 45 C.F.R. §400.115(c).

3. Literature that may be helpful in the area of teen access to reproductive care includes English, A. *et al*, State Minor Consent Statutes: A Summary, Nat. Ctr. For Youth Law (S.F.CA, 1995); English, A. *et al*, Adolescents in Public Health Insurance Programs: Medicaid and CHIP, Ctr. for Adolescent Health & the Law (Chapel Hill, N.C. , 1999); Veith, S., *The Judicial Bypass Procedure and Adolescent's Abortion Rights*, 32 Hofstra L.Rev. 453 (1994); Donovan, P. (1997), Teenagers fight to consent to reproductive health care, The Alan Guttmacher Institute, http://www.agii-usa.org.

4. E.g. Bergman, A.B., *The shame of foster care health services*, Arch. Pediatr. Adolesc. Med. 2000, 154:1080-1; Roman, N.P., Wolfe P.B. *The relationship between foster care and homelessness*. Public Welfare 1997:55:4-3; Halfon, *et al*, *Mental health service utilization by children in foster care in California*. Pediatrics 1992; 89:1238-44; English, A. *et al*, *Access to health care for youth leaving foster care: Medicaid and Schip*, Journal of Adolescent Health, June 2003, 32:6, 53-69.

5. Other states that have enacted foster parents rights laws include Maryland, Maryland Family Law Article §5-504; Illinois, Illinois Compiled Stat. Ann. Chap. 20, Dep't of Child and Family Services Article 1, Sec. 1-15 (20 ILCS 520/1-15 (2004); Mississippi, Miss Code Ann. § 43-15-13 (2004) Title 43. Public Welfare, Chap. 15, Child Welfare, Article 1; Oklahoma, 10 Okl. St. §7206.1 (2002) Title 10 Children Chap 72; Washington, Rev. Code Wash ARCW §74.13.332 (2004) Title 74, Public Assistance, Chap. 74.13 Child Welfare Services Foster Care.

6. *See also Marylou v. Tenecha L.*, 698 N.Y.S.2d 827 (Fam. Ct. 1999)(Foster parent does not have standing to seek custody of child in foster care); *In the interest of G.C.*, 673 A.2d 932 (Pa. Super 1996) (Foster parents do not have standing to challenge custody decisions); *Bingenheimer v. Wisc. Dept. of Health and Human Serv.*, 383 N.W. 2d 898, (Wisc. 1986)(Wisconsin law creates a right of foster parents to participate in and present evidence in hearings involving the "placement and care" of foster children).

7. Lower federal courts remain divided on the application of *Smith v.O.F.F.E.R..* Holding that foster parents do not have a right to a relationship are *Procopio v. Johnson,* 994 F. 2d 325 (7th Cir. 1993), *Wildauer v. Frederick County,* 993 F. 2d 369 (4th Cir. 1993); and *Keyes v. County Dep't of Pub. Welfare of Tippecanoe County,* 600 F. 2d 693 (7th Cir. 1979). *Spielman v. Hildebrand,* 873 F. 2d 1377 (10th Cir. 1989) held that foster parents have an interest in a relationship but that the removal procedures did not violate due process. For other cases finding that a protected interest exists *see Rivera v. Marcus,* 696 F.2d 1016 (2d Cir. 1982); *Thelen v. Catholic Soc. Servs.,* 691 F. Supp. 1179 (E.D.Wis. 1988); *Brown v. County of San Joaquin,* 601 F. Supp. 653 (E.D. Cal. 1985).

8. *Smith v. State of Louisiana,* 452 So.2d 388 (La.Ct.App. 3rd Cir. 1984) (A foster parent does not have a legally recognized right to their foster child); *In the Interest of G.C., A Minor Child, Appeal of M.S. and B.S.,* 735 A.2d 1226 (Pa. 1999) (Foster parents do not have standing to contest custody decision affecting foster children); *In re Guardianship of P.J.D.,* 600 P.2d 1170 (Mont. 1979)(Foster parents cannot petition for guardianship when the rights of the biological parents have been terminated and it is the state agency that has "permanent legal custody with the right to consent to the adoption. …"); *Division of Family Services v. Harrison,* 741 A.2d 1016 (DE. 1999) (Foster parents have authority to seek guardianship without agency consent); *In re Review of Foster Care Status of Melissa M.,* 421 N.Y.S.2d 300 (Fam. Ct. 1979) (Foster parents' motion for visitation with former foster child denied); *In re Marilyn H.,* 436 N.Y.S.2d 814 (Fam. Ct. 1981) (Foster parents can initiate termination of parental rights to obtain guardianship).

9. Evidentiary standards describe how much evidence is required for the court to find that the state has proved its case. These vary somewhat from state to state. Three standards frequently occurring are 1) "probable cause" at the shelter care hearing (more probable than not that the event occurred), 2) "preponderance of the evidence" at the trial (more than 50% likely that the event occurred), and 3) "clear and convincing evidence" at the termination of parental rights hearing (just short of "beyond a reasonable doubt).

10. E.g. Texas Family Code Ann. Sec.107.013:
(a) In a suit in which termination of the parent-child relationship is requested, the court shall appoint an attorney *ad litem* to represent the interests of (1) an indigent parent of the child who responds in opposition to the termination; (2) a parent served by citation by publication; (3) an alleged father who failed to register with the registry under Chapter 160 and whose identity or location is unknown; and (4) an alleged father who registered with the paternity registry under Chapter 160 , but the petitioner's attempt to personally serve citation at the address provided to the registry and at any other address for the alleged father known by the petitioner is unsuccessful.
(b) if both parents of the child are entitled to the appointment of an attorney *ad litem* under this section and the court finds that the interests of the parents are not in conflict, the court may appoint a single attorney *ad litem* to represent the interests of both parents.

11. E.g. Cal.Welf.& Inst.Code § 317:
(b) When it appears to the court that a parent or guardian of the child is presently financially unable to afford and cannot for that reason employ counsel, and the child

has been placed in out-of-home care, or the petitioning agency is recommending that the child be placed in out of home care, the court shall appoint counsel, unless the court finds that the parent or guardian has made a knowing and intelligent waiver of counsel as provided in this section.

12. Foster care can be delivered by nongovernmental entities, usually nonprofit faith-based organizations. This aspect of foster care is covered in Chapter Five. It is also possible for foster care to be provided without any government involvement at all. This situation would be a totally private arrangement between a parent and a provider to care for a child in a home-like environment. These situations, which are beyond the scope of this book, are very rare and would be analogous to sending a child to a boarding school or to a residential facility.

13. This book does not address other types of placements such as group homes and congregate care, hospitals or residential and psychiatric facilities.

14. Even when parental rights have been extinguished there is some debate over whether the rights of the government are identical to the parents. The answer seems to be no. There are limits to state authority and exceeding this authority would require court involvement. *Parham v. J.R.*, 442 U.S. 584 (1979), a case involving the state's authority to admit foster children into a mental health facility, is the Supreme Court opinion that sets limits on agency decision-making for children in state custody.

15. For additional discussion of this topic see Appendix A Section II.

16. The Uniform Child Custody Jurisdiction and Enforcement Act (UCCJEA) also addresses interstate "dependency" matters. E.g., Jackson v. The Superior Court of San Diego County, 130 Cal. Rptr. 2d 502 (Ct.App. 2003) (Placement into foster care is a child custody determination under the UCCJEA).

17. The U.S. Department of Health and Human Services Administration for Children and Families issues detailed policies and guidelines regarding the use of federal funds for foster care. Court cases involving funding and eligibility issues are rare but have significant impact on state spending. E.g. *Capitola Land v. Anderson*, 63 Cal. Rptr. 2d 717 (Ct.App. 1997)(Children qualified for federal foster care payments despite contrary regulations issued by state Department of Social Services); *Miller v. Youakim*, 440 U.S. 125 (1979) (Improper to deny benefits to children residing with relatives); *California Dep't of Social Services v. Thompson*, 321 F.3d 835 (9th Cir. 2003)(State must make foster care payments to relatives caring for foster children) reversing *California Dep't of Social Services v. Shalala*, 115 F.Supp. 2d 1191 (E.D. Ca. 2000).

18. These and other confidentiality-related statutes have been collected by the National Child Welfare Resource Center on Legal and Judicial Issues at the American Bar Association Center for Children and the Law. See, M. Hardin, "Privacy and Information Sharing in Child Welfare cases," http://www.abanet.org/child/ncXXX/privacy-case.pdf. Or contact markhardin@staff.abanet.org. The Children's Bureau at the U.S. Health and Human Services Administration has issued some helpful policy guidance about what information can be released to the public and what can be discussed in open court. www.acf.hhs.gov, Policy Guidance No. ACYF-CB-PIQ-98-01.

19. Every foster care agency should have policies and procedures to comply with HIPAA. One issue that will be important to foster care is whether it is state law or HIPAA that applies to certain disclosures, such as the disclosure of a foster child's health information to a foster or biological parent. See Jennifer Guthrie, Time is Running Out—The Burdens and Challenges of HIPAA Compliance: A Look at Preemption Analysis, the "Minimum Necessary" Standard and the Notice of Privacy Practices, 12 Ann. Health L. 143 (2003).

20. *See S.C. v Guardian ad Litem,* 845 So.2d 953 (Fl.Ct.App.2003) (Child in shelter care had right to notice and opportunity to be heard to prevent disclosure of therapeutic records to guardian *ad litem*); *J.P. v. DeSanti,* 653 F.2d 1080 (6th Cir. 1981) (Dissemination of social histories of juvenile offenders); *Pennsylvania v. Ritchie,* 480 U.S. 39 (1987) (Disclosure of child abuse records in a criminal proceedings); *S.M. by R.M. v. Children and Youth Services of Delaware County,* 686 A.2d 872 (Pa. Cmwlth. 1996) (Foster child, parents and legal guardian were entitled to family case record of foster family in which child was allegedly abused); *Matter of Damon A.R.,* 447 N.Y.S.2d 237 (N.Y.Fam.Ct. 1982) (Child subject to a neglect investigation has statutory right to access to reports made to child protective services); *Nevada Division of Child and Family Services, Department of Human Resources v. The Eighth Judicial District Court of the State of Nevada, in and for the County of Clark,* 81 P.3d 512 (Nev. 2003)(Denial of minor child's attempt to obtain names of sibling's adoptive and biological parents).

21. http://www.cfsa.dc.gov/cfsa/frames.asp?doc=/cfsa/lib/cfsa/frames/pdf/family-based _rfp3.pdf.

22. At present foster care is delivered by foster homes that are attached to an agency—either a public or private foster care agency. This agency provides the monitoring, supervision, and on-going training. Almost always it is this same agency that created the foster home resource by recruiting, training, and "certifying" the foster home. It is possible to envision a system in which individuals can somehow become licensed without applying to or becoming attached to a particular agency. These "freelance" foster parents, with license in hand, would offer their services to a particular agency (or to the agency that offers the "best" benefits). Of course once the agency accepts the "freelance" foster parents, it has the responsibility to assure compliance with all relevant standards, determine if the home were a suitable placement for a particular child, and assure that any child placed is receiving good care. Thus, this "freelance" approach would not be much different than the current system.

23. Cases dealing with public foster care agencies: *Stanley by Stanley v. State Indus., Inc.,* 630 A. 2d 1188 (N.J. Super. Ct.L.Div. 1993) (State lacked sufficient control over foster parents to make them agents or employees of the state and therefore the state could not be liable for foster parents' negligence); *Hunte v. Blumenthal,* 680 A.2d 1231 (Conn.1996) (Foster parents are state employees); *Simmons v. Robinson,* 409 S.E. 2d 381 (S.C. 1991) (Foster parents are not employees of state agency); *Mitzner v. Kansas,* 891 P.2d 435 (Kan. 1995) (foster parents are independent contractors). Cases dealing with private foster care agencies: *Commerce Bank v. Youth Services of Mid-Illinois, Inc.,*787 N.E.2d 171 (Ill. App. 2002) (Foster parents are independent contractors); *L.G. v. Barber,* C-8-99-258, Court of Appeals of Minnesota, July 20, 1999 (unpublished), 1999 Minn. App. LEXIS 839 (Whether or not a foster parent is an employee or an independent contractor is a fact issue).

24. Some federal laws that particularly affect neglect-abuse practice are: *The Adoption and Safe Families Act of 1997*,P.L. 105-89, 42 U.S.C. §§620-679; *Early and Periodic Screening, Diagnostic and Treatment Services, the Medicaid Act,* 42 U.S.C. §§1396(a)(43); 1396(d)(a)(4)(B), 1396 (d)(r); *The Individuals with Disabilities Education Act of 1975 as amended 1997,* P.L. 105-17; 20 U.S.C. §1401 *et seq; The Foster Care Independence Act of 1999,* P.L. 106-169, 42 U.S.C. §677 *et seq; The Americans with Disabilities Act of 1990*,P.L. 101-336, 42 U.S.C. §121-1 *et seq; The Child Abuse Prevention and Treatment Act*,P.L. 100-294, 42 U.S.C. §51006a as amended 2003; *The Multi-Ethnic Placement Act*,P.L. 103-382, Title V, Part E, 42 U.S.C. §1996b; *The Indian Child Welfare Act of 1978*,P.L.95-608; 25 U.S.C. §§1901-1963.

25. In a few cases a private agency employee might appear with the private agency's attorney, who would not be a government attorney. That might occur if there were a conflict between the government and the private agency. Normally, such a dispute would be separated from the foster care case.

26. An exception occurs in family drug courts. A few court systems offer parents with drug problems a chance to enter drug treatment under court supervision, thereby increasing their chance to reunite with their child. Some family drug courts require participants to consent to incarceration for failing drug tests and other violations of the treatment protocol.

27. "Title IV-E requires, as a condition of eligibility, that a child's placement and care responsibility be vested either with the state agency, or another public agency with which the state has an agreement. The purpose of the regulatory provision in question is to assure that the authority of the state title IV-E agency with placement and care responsibility for the child is not usurped. A "court-ordered" placement, as prohibited in the rule, involves the court taking placement and care responsibility away from the agency and assuming placement and care responsibility by choosing the child's placement without *bona fide* consideration of the agency's recommendation regarding placement. This does not mean that the court must always concur with the agency's recommendation in order for the child to be eligible for title IV-E foster care payments. As long as the court hears the relevant testimony and works with all parties, including the agency with placement and care responsibility, to make appropriate placement decisions, we will not disallow the payments. The prohibition in the rule also does not apply to situations where the court merely names the child's placement in the court order as an endorsement or approval of the agency's placement choice." HHS official interpretation of ASFA regulations.

28. In Virginia a disposition order is appealable, 16-2-278.2A.7.(D) Illinois defines the permanency order as final, *In re Curtis B.,* 784 N.E. 2d 219 (Ill.2002). In North Carolina "any order modifying custodial rights" can be appealed, *In re Weiler,* 581 S.E.2d 134 (NC 2003). That is also true in California if the order passes an initial test, CA Welf.&Inst.Code A7-395; *In re Meranda P.,* 65 Cal Rptr.2d 913 (1997). Pennsylvania agrees, permitting appeal whenever there is a goal change, *In re C.J.R.,* 782 A.2d 568, 569 (Pa.Super.2001). In Maine appealable orders are the disposition following adjudication, medical treatment orders, and TPRs, ME Rev.Stat.Ann.Title 20-4035, 4054, 4071.

29. South Dakota law states "Foster parents shall be liable for personal injuries sustained by foster children only to the extent natural parents are liable to their children." S.D.

Codified Laws Title 25 Chapter 25-5 §25-5-23. Washington has a similar law which states " In actions for personal injury or property damage committed by foster children or their parents against foster parents licensed [under Washington law] the liability of foster parents for the care and supervision of foster children shall be the same as the liability of biological and adoptive parents for the care and supervision of their children. Washington St. §4.24.590.

30.   [The law] also provides that an agency that acts in good faith in placing a child with the foster parent will also be immune from civil liability for any act or omission of the agency, the foster parent or the foster child. The immunity does not apply if: (a) the agency fails to provide the foster parent with any information it possesses or reasonably should possess relating to medical, physical or emotional conditions of the foster child…and (b) bodily injury to the child or any other person or damage to the property of the child or any other person is a direct result of that failure.

31. Indemnification is similar in effect to reimbursement. If a foster parent has to pay an attorney to defend her against a lawsuit, or has to pay damages as a result of a suit, she could be indemnified, or paid back, by the government.

32. Indemnification does not cover intentional or criminal acts.

33. Alaska law indemnifies for injuries occurring "during the performance and within the scope of duty of the foster care program". Alaska does not indemnify for intentional misconduct. Alaska Admin Code tit. 7, § 51.110 (1997). Florida immunizes agencies, Fla. Admin Code Ann r. 65-B.6.009 but has general liability insurance for those who provide foster care. Fla Stat Ann §393.075. How Florida's legislatively mandated privatization of foster care will affect liability is an unanswered question.

34. Maine has a law providing for insurance for foster homes which includes a clause that the law does not "make the operation of a family foster home a state activity nor may it expand in any way the liability of the state or foster parent." Maine Rev Stat Ann Title 22, Subtitle 6, Chap 1669 §8101. Maryland has a law stating that the state shall provide "liability insurance for foster parents who care for children under foster parent programs. This fund responds to claims by foster children against foster parents and bodily injury and property damage by the foster child to the foster parent that insurance does not cover. Family Law Art 5-529. Nebraska has a similar law, Neb §43-905 43-1320, as does New Hampshire Title XII Chap 170-G:3. Washington also has a foster parent liability insurance program (74.14B.080) and also provides for the defense of foster parents who have been sued, 4.92.060. (For a case involving the California foster care fund see *Rodriguez v. Superior Court of Los Angeles County*, 108 Cal. App 4th 301, 133 Cal. Rptr. 2d 294 (2003).For commentary on this issue see D. Pollack, *Liability Insurance for Foster Parents and Agencies: The Role of Commercial Insurers*, 4 Journal of Law & Social Work 1, (May 1993) and Cavanaugh and Pollack, *Liability Protection for Foster Parents*, 6 Kan. J.L. & Pub. Policy 78 (1997).

35. For another case involving insurance and foster children see *Cadwallader v. Allstate Insurance Co.*, 848 So.2d 577 (La. 2003)(Foster child is not a "resident relative" as that term is used in an automobile insurance policy)..

36. Although rare, there are occasions when foster parents buy or try to buy life insurance for their foster child. *Willingham v. United Insurance Co. of America,* 628 So. 2d 328 (Ala. 1993) (Foster parents do not have insurable interest in foster child).

37. "Vicarious liability" is a legal term meaning that one person is liable for the acts of another.

38. In Arizona parents and legal guardians, but not foster parents, are civilly liable for shoplifting by unemancipated minors. Arizona Revised Statutes 12-692. Several other states have similar laws. E.g. New Jersey NJSA 2A:61C-1. New Mexico imposes liability on biological parents if the child has "maliciously or willfully" caused injury or damage, but "nothing in this [law] shall be construed so as to impute liability to any foster parent". New Mexico, 32A-2-27. Oregon has a very similar laws Or. Rev. Stat. §30-765.

39. An agency is not a guarantor of anyone's safety or well being. Not all injuries will result in liability to the agency or its employees. That is, the agency is not responsible for accidents but for its negligence. The agency may be responsible for ameliorating the harm of an accidental injury and may be required to insure itself against accidents. For example, if a foster child falls down the stairs in a foster home the agency must see to it that the child gets medical attention. But the agency cannot be sued just because a child fell down the stairs.

40. Statutes and regulations can themselves create liability. When analyzing such statutes it is important to determine whether or not the language supposedly imposing liability is explicit and mandatory. In other words, does the law prescribe and mandate compliance with specific procedures which limit the discretion of the social worker? For instance, does the law prescribe a certain minimum number of home visits? Sometimes, however, even when it appears that the agency's procedures were not followed, liability is avoided because a statute did not mandate the services. *County of Los Angeles v. the Superior Court of Los Angeles County,* 125 Cal.Rptr 2d 637 (Ct. App 2002) ("A county social worker is immune from liability for negligent supervision of a foster child unless the social worker fails to provide specific services mandated by stature or regulation". Citations omitted).

41. For a case in which expert testimony regarding the standard of care applicable to the agency's selection and monitoring of a foster parent was required see *District of Columbia v. Hampton,* 666 A.2d 30 (D.C. 1995). For another case involving standards see *Doe by and through G.S. v. Johnson,* 52 F.3d 1448 (7th Cir. 1995)(Expert testimony regarding standard of care for supervision of foster child's placement in foster home).

42. The literature explaining and interpreting *Deshaney* and its effect on government agency liability for foster children and others is extensive. A good introductory article is Michelle Miller, *Revisiting Poor Joshua: State-Created Danger Theory in the Foster Care Context,* 11 Hastings Women's Law Journal 243 (2000).

43. *Commerce Bank v. Youth Services of Mid-Illinois,Inc.,* 775 N.E.2d 297, (App. Ct. Ill. 2002) (Foster parent is an independent contractor and not an employee); *Simmons v. Robinson,* 409 S.E.2d 381 (SC 1991) (State Department of Social Services not vicariously liable for injuries to foster child because foster parent was not an agent or employee but a "mere licensee"). However, sometimes the result is the opposite. See for

example, *Bartels v. Westchester County,* 429 N.Y.S. 2d 906 (Supreme Ct. App. Div.1980). (The duty of the agency to supervise the foster parent creates principal-agent relationship resulting in liability to the agency).

44. The immunity relevant to suits under federal civil rights law 42 U.S.C. §1983 is discussed in Section IV.D.

45. For other cases see *Johnson v. State,* 447 P.2d 352, (CA. 1968) (State had a duty to inform the foster mother of information that might endanger the foster parents and family). *Snyder v. Mouser,* 272 N,E.2d 627 (Ind. 1971)(State is liable for failure to warn of foster child's homicidal propensities);*Haselhart v. State,* 485 N.W.2d 180 (Neb. 1992)(State had a duty to discover and disclose information regarding foster child's violent history.) There are two other duty to disclose cases that were dismissed based on immunity of the state agency. Therefore, they do not assist in determining when a failure to disclose will lead to liability. However, the facts illustrate the kinds of circumstances that can give rise to a duty to disclose. In one case the foster child had a known history of sexual abuse and subsequently abused the foster parents' own children. *M.D.R. v. State ex. rel. Human Services Dep't,* 836 P.2d 106 (N.M.App. 1992). In another case the foster mother alleged that the defendant state agency and others knew that the foster mother intended to become pregnant and were negligent in placing into her home a child who was a carrier of cytomegalic inclusion disease, a disease which can cause defects in an unborn fetus. The foster mother got pregnant, contracted the disease, and a doctor recommended abortion. *Vaughn v. County of Durham,* 240 S.E.2d 456 (1977) cert den 241 S.E.2d 522 (N.C. 1978.)

46. A similar argument had been rejected in *Dorothy J. v. Little Rock School District,* 794 F. Supp. 1405 (E.D. Ark. 1992) in which it was decided that being a ward of the state does not make a child a state actor for liability purposes.

47. For a case in which a foster child was sexually abused by another foster child but whose federal claims under 42 U.S.C. §1983 based on a failure to adhere to state law were dismissed, see *Coker on behalf of Coker v. Henry,* 813 F. Supp. 567 (W.D. MI. 1993).

48. One recent class action suit is *Braam ex rel. Braam v. Washington,* 81 P.3d 851 (Wash. 2003).

49. There are many §1983 cases related to foster care and the literature in this area is extensive. For a comprehensive legal analysis of §1983 and the legal standards employed in such cases see Brendan P. Kearse, *Abused Again: Competing Constitutional Standards for the State's Duty to Protect Foster Children,* 29 Columbia. J. L. & Soc. Probs. 385 (1996). *Doe v. New York City Dep't of Soc. Servs.,* 649 F.2d 134, 136-7 (2d Cir. 1981) 709 F.2d 782(2 Cir.1983) cert den 464 U.S. 864 (Claiming violation of substantive due process under § 1983 for injuries suffered through rape, beatings, and other forms of child abuse while in foster care). *Doe* is the earliest federal circuit court case regarding foster care agency-foster parent liability. Other important foster care cases would include *Norfleet v. Ark. Dep't of Human Servs.,* 989 F.2d at 289 (8 Cir. 1993) (Claiming violation of substantive due process under § 1983 for deprivation of life as a result of indifference to medical needs of foster child); *Yvonne L. v. N.M. Dep't of Human Servs.,* 959 F.2d 883, 885 (10 Cir. 1992) (Claiming violation of substantive due process

under § 1983 for failure to protect child from bodily harm when placed by state in private crisis shelter group home); *K.H. ex rel. Murphy v. Morgan,* 914 F.2d 846, 847-8 (7th Cir. 1990) (Claiming violation of substantive due process under § 1983 for neglect while in foster care); *Meador v. Cabinet for Human Res.,* 902 F.2d 474, 475 (6th Cir. 1990) (Claiming violation of procedural and substantive due process under § 1983 for sexual abuse of children while under the state's care); *Taylor ex rel. Walker v. Ledbetter,* 818 F.2d 791 (11 Cir. 1987) (Permanent injuries suffered by child while in foster care). *L.J. v. Massinga,* 838 F.2d 118, (4 Cir. 1984) later proceeding 699 F.Supp 508 (D. Md. 1988), cert. den. 488 U.S. 1018 (1989)(Evidence showed agency failed to protect foster children when there was reason to know children were at risk of harm); *T.M. v. Carson,*93 F. Supp 2d 1179 (D.Wy 2000) (Children abused in home where foster father had a history of sexual harassment sexually assaultive behavior and sexual abuse.)*Hernandez v. Texas Department of Protective and Regulatory Services,* 2002 U.S. Dist LEXIS 22707, 2002 W.L. 31689710 is a very interesting and useful discussion of the duty to train and duty to supervise.

50. *Daniels v. Williams,* 474 U.S. 327, (1986)(Negligence); *Archie v. City of Racine,* 847 F. 2d 1211 (7th Cir. 1988)(en banc) (Gross negligence), cert. denied, 489 U.S. 1065 (1989).

51. The professional judgment standard traces its roots to *Youngberg v. Romero,* 457 US 307, 323 (1982), which concluded that a decision made by a professional is "presumptively valid; liability may be imposed only when the decision by the professional is such a substantial departure from accepted professional judgment, practice or standards as to demonstrate that the person responsible actually did not base the decision on such judgment".

52. *T.M.* involved children abused in a home where the foster father had a history of sexual harassment, sexually assaultive behavior, and sexual abuse. He was eventually convicted of 12 counts of sexual assault for his abuse of the foster children.

53. Deliberate indifference is the standard of liability applied in the Second, Third, Fourth, Sixth, Eighth, Ninth, Tenth, and Eleventh Circuits. *See Roska v. Peterson,* 304 F.3d 982, 994 (10th Cir. 2002) (Applying the deliberate indifference standard in a case involving a child in foster care); *Nicini v. Morra,* 212 F.3d 798, 811 (3d Cir. 2000) (Determining deliberate indifference to be the correct standard by which to judge actions of a state agency and caseworker in the case of a child abused while in foster care); *Norfleet ex rel. Norfleet v. Ark. Dep't of Human Servs.,* 989 F.2d 289, 293 (8th Cir. 1993) (Using the deliberate indifference standard in a case claiming liability of a state agency and officials for a child's death as a result of not receiving medical attention for asthma while in temporary foster care); *Meador v. Cabinet for Human Res.,* 902 F.2d 474, 476 (6th Cir. 1990) (Using the deliberate indifference standard in a case involving children sexually abused while in foster care); *Taylor ex rel. Walker v. Ledbetter,*818 F.2d 791, 792 (11th Cir. 1987) (Using the deliberate indifference standard in a case involving a child left comatose after abuse by foster mother); *Doe v. New York City Dep't of Soc. Servs.,* 649 F.2d 134, 137 (2d Cir. 1981) (Using deliberate indifference standard in a case involving physical and sexual abuse in foster care). Professional judgment is the standard of liability applied in the Seventh Circuit. *See K. H. ex rel. Murphy v. Morgan,* 914 F.2d 846, 848 (7th Cir. 1990) (Using professional judgment standard in a case

involving abuse of a child in two different foster homes). *Yvonne L. v. N.M. Dep't of Human Servs.*, 959 F.2d 883, 894 (10th Cir. 1992) (Applying the professional judgment standard in a case involving a child sexually assaulted by another minor in a nonsupervised area of a foster care group home); *Winston v. Children & Youth Servs. Of Del. County,*948 F.2d 1380, 1390 (3d Cir. 1991) (Applying the professional judgment standard in a case of a challenge by natural parents to the visitation policy of the agency).

54. When foster children are injured by foster parents the first question to be asked is whether or not the injury was intentional (such as a physical assault or sexual molestation), negligent, or accidental. *J.H. v. Johnson,* 346 F.3d 788 (7th Cir. 2003), a case in which children were injured by their foster fathers, is also a case that demonstrates how difficult it is to prove that a state agency is liable even when it cannot be doubted that children are abused by foster parents. This case is especially useful in explaining the differing and competing standards used to determine when liability will attach. In this case the court ruled that the children failed to show that the state agency and the caseworkers knew or should have known that the children were at risk for child abuse. This case employed the deliberate indifference standard which requires proof that the social workers knew or suspected a specific risk and consciously ignored it or failed to stop it.

55. Examples of cases that address the immunity of social workers in the context of the liability of state foster care agencies include *Whitley v. New Mexico Children, Youth & Families Department,* 184 F. Supp. 2d 1146 (D. N.M. 2001) (Discusses both qualified immunity related to 1983 and sovereign immunity under New Mexico law for claims under state law). See also, *Pickett v. Washington County,* 572 P.2d 1070 (Or. App. 1977); *Lintz v. Skipski,* 815 F.Supp 1066 (W.D. Mich. 1993) (Focusing on the "clearly established aspect of establishing immunity), *Roes v. Florida Department of Children and Family Services,* 176 F. Supp. 2d 1310 (S.D. Fl. 2001) (Example of how social worker's actions can impact immunity).

56. *Rayburn v. Hogue,* 241 F.3d 1341 (11th Cir. 2001)(Foster parents are not state actors); *K.H. ex. rel. Murphy v. Morgan,* 914 F.2d 846 (7th Cir. 1990)(Foster parents even if paid by the state are not state agents for constitutional purposes). *Millburn v. Anne Arundel County Dep't of Soc.Servs.,* 871 F.2d 474 (4th Cir. 1989). (Foster parents are not state actors); *Pfoltzer v. County of Fairfax,* 775 F. Supp. 874 (E.D. Va. 1991)(Foster parents are not state actors).

57. *Donlan v. Ridge,* 58 F.Supp.2d 604 (E.D. Pa. 1999) tentatively concludes that a private foster care agency is a "state actor" and contains a brief but useful discussion of cases relevant to "state actor status" and private foster care agencies. *Malachowski v.City of Keene,* 787 F.2d 704 (1st Cir. 1986) (Private nonprofit foster care agency did not "assume state's mantle of authority" and was not therefore acting under color of state law). *Estate of Adam Earp v. Mary Ann Doud, et al.* 1997 U.S. Dist. LEXIS 6702 (E.D. Pa. Civil Action No. 96-7141 5/7/97).(Private foster care agency is a state actor for §1983 purposes). Even if a private agency is not liable under §1983 this does not mean it cannot be held accountable for its actions. It may still be sued under state negligence law. For a case not involving §1983 but addressing "governmental actor" issues see *Tyler v. Children's Home Society,* 35 Cal. Rptr. 2d 291 (Cal Ct. App 1994) (Private

licensed adoption agency is "an agent of the state" and "is a governmental actor for purposes of due process analysis").

58. There are very few cases that address the relationship between a private actor being found to be a state actor and the ability to claim the protections afforded by qualified immunity that a "state actor" could claim. For two cases addressing state actor and immunity issue, although not in a foster care context, see *Tewksbury v. Dowling,* 169 F.Supp. 2d 103 (E.D. NY 2001) and *Jensen v. Lane County,* 222 F.3d 570 (9th Cir. 2000). For a case involving a private child welfare - foster care agency, but not involving an injury to a foster child, see *Bartell v. Lohiser,* 215 F.3d 550 (6th Cir. 2000). See also, *Warner v. Grand County,* 57 F.3d 962 (10th Cir. 1995)(Qualified immunity is available to private defendant), *Sherman v. Four County Counseling Center,* 987 F.2d 397 (7th Cir. 1993) (Qualified immunity is available to a private corporation). But see,*Campbell v. City of Philadelphia Dep't of Human Services,* 1990 WL 102945 (E.D.Pa 1990) (Private agency is a state actor for §1983 purposes but is not entitled to claim §1983 immunity from punitive damages).

59. *Thornton v. Commonwealth,* 552 N.E.2d 601, (Mass App 1990). In this case the court relied upon a statute that allowed contracting for services. It is possible that in a jurisdiction where there was no statutory authority to contract the result could be different.

Glossary of Terms

Acronyms and Abbreviations

ASFA	Adoption and Safe Families Act
CAPTA	Child Abuse Prevention and Treatment Act
CASA	Court Appointed Special Advocate
CFR	Code of Federal Regulations
DSM-IV-R	Diagnostic and Statistical Manual, 4th Ed., revised
EPSDT	Early and Periodic Screening, Diagnostic and Treatment Services
FFP	federal financial participation
FERPA	Family Education Rights and Privacy Act
F.R.	Federal Register (a government publication)
HIPAA	Health Insurance Portability Accountability Act
ICPC	Interstate Compact on the Placement of Children
ICWA	Indian Child Welfare Act
IDEA	Individuals with Disabilities Education Act
IEP	Individual Education Plan
SCHIP	State Child's Health Insurance Program
SSA	Social Security Act
SSI	Supplemental Security Income
TPR	termination of parental rights
USC	United States Code
501(c)(3)	nonprofit tax-exempt agency

Words and Phrases

Adjudication: Trial.

Allegation: An unproved charge.

Appeal: Complaint to a higher court by a losing party, alleging that the trial court's decision was in error.

Best interests of the child: An important judicial standard for deciding foster care and other family cases. Elements that make up "best interests" may, or may not, be defined in a state's case law or statutes.

Beyond a reasonable doubt: the highest evidentiary standard, usually applicable in criminal felony cases, but also found in the ICWA.

Biological parents: birth parents.

Civil law: disputes that do not involve criminal acts are resolved under civil law. Most neglect-abuse cases are governed by civil laws in family and juvenile courts, though criminal acts of neglect-abuse that result in criminal charges are tried in criminal courts.

Claiming: a process used by state agencies to justify entitlement to federal payment for services provided to families and children.

Clear and convincing: a high standard of evidence applied at the critical stage of termination of parental rights. It is applied differently in the ICWA.

Compelling reason: an ASFA term referring to a reason strong enough to overcome an otherwise applicable law. E.g. At the permanency hearing a child is to be placed in one of four permanent placements within a certain time frame, unless the judge finds there is a "compelling reason" to make another arrangement.

Dependency: the state of being dependent on government support

Dependency court: a civil court in which neglect-abuse cases are heard.

Dependent child: under federal law, a child who receives 24-hour out-of-home care, supported by government funds.

Discovery: a legal process for obtaining documents and information about a case.

Disposition: a stage of the case at which court orders are issued about where a child shall stay and what services shall be offered. Dispositions can be temporary or permanent.

Due process: a bundle of legal rights available to an individual through the 14th Amendment to the U.S. Constitution, including notice, cross-examination, learning the facts against one, and the opportunity to present one's own case.

Duty of care: a high standard of care required by law of some persons and entities like foster care agencies. It is a duty to avoid negligent behavior.

Duty to disclose: a legal obligation to provide information.

Emergency placement: swift removal of a child from parents where dangerous circumstances do not leave time for a prior court order or hearing.

Evidentiary standards: phrases that describe the amount of evidence needed to convince a court of an alleged situation. E.g. probable cause, preponderance, clear and convincing, and beyond a reasonable doubt.

Guardian *ad litem:* a guardian at law, not a custodial guardian.

Immunity: a legal principle that provides an exemption from civil lawsuits.

In loco parentis: "in place of the parents."

Indemnification: reimbursement for a loss.

Independent contractor: a person whose services are obtained by contract for particular projects. An independent contractor exercises independent judgment, as compared to an employee who takes direction from an employer.

Indigent person: a person without funds to pay for services.

Interlocutory: prior to a final order.

Jurisdiction: authority of the court to consider and decide cases.

Kinship care: care provided by a child's relatives.

Legal custody: a judicially-granted authority and responsibility to care for another person, usually a child.

Legal guardianship: Under ASFA, a judicially-created relationship between a child and a caretaker, meant to be permanent, transferring certain parental rights to the guardian, including protection, education, care and control, custody and decision-making.

Legal interests: interests protected by law, such as rights to receive notice of a legal proceeding, obtain documents, and present witnesses.

Matching funds: a formula for determining federal payments to states based on state spending.

Motions: a legal process to petition the court to decide a particular issue.

Multi-jurisdictional: the laws and authorities of more than one state apply to the case.

Negligence (liability): conduct falling below the standard established to protect people from harm.

Neighborhood collaboratives: a collective of organizations working together to address the concerns of a particular community.

Notice: notification that the recipient is, or has the opportunity to be, a participant in a legal process.

Parent: neglect-abuse cases can involve guardians, adoptive parents, and other custodial adults, in place of the birth parents. In this book the term "parent" extends to other adults charged with neglect-abuse, except where the constitutional rights of birth parents are referenced.

Party: a person by, or against whom, a lawsuit is brought; also, persons named as parties by statute or rule, or declared parties by the court because their interests are directly affected by the action.

Petition: a legal document requesting a court to take jurisdiction over a case, or to resolve a particular legal issue.

Placement: living arrangement.

Preponderance of evidence: more than 50% of the evidence.

Privatize: to turn over a governmental function, like management of foster care, to a private entity.

Probable cause: a standard of evidence: it is more probable than not that an event occurred.

Reasonable efforts: an ASFA phrase referring to the amount of effort that a foster care agency must make toward accomplishing the child's permanency goal.

Relinquishment: consent to give up rights, as in relinquishment of parental rights so that a child can be adopted.

Residual parental rights: those rights retained by parents while their child is in foster care custody, usually thought to include major medical decisions, religion, and education.

Respondeat superior: in law, a concept that the "master" may be responsible for the acts of a "servant." Eg. a foster care agency may be responsible for negligent acts of a foster parent.

Shelter care: an initial placement of the child away from home, prior to adjudication of the facts.

Speedy trial: a statutory requirement in some states than an adjudication occur within a few weeks of the initial removal of the child from the parent.

Standard of care: the quality of care that should be delivered.

Standing: a party's right to make a legal claim or seek judicial enforcement of a duty or right.

Stipulated agreement: an agreement between the parents and government about the facts of a case.

Subsidized guardianship: legal guardianship made possible by financial or other support (for example, Medicaid) from the government.

Testamentary evidence: oral evidence by a witness of facts related to a case.

Unaccompanied minors: refugee children who arrive in the U.S. without an accompanying adult.

Vicarious liability: a supervisor's liability for the negligent behavior of a subordinate.

Voluntary placement: placement of a child in foster care by willing parents, as contrasted with removal of a child against parental wishes.

INDEX